With Love From Heaven

With Love From Heaven

◆

Even Death Can't Separate Us from the Ones We Love

Catherine A. Roberts

iUniverse, Inc.
New York Lincoln Shanghai

With Love From Heaven
Even Death Can't Separate Us from the Ones We Love

iUniverse, Inc.

For information address:
iUniverse, Inc.
2021 Pine Lake Road, Suite 100
Lincoln, NE 68512
www.iuniverse.com

ISBN: 0-595-30434-6

Printed in the United States of America

This book is dedicated to the following people, all of whom have immeasurable and lasting importance in my life.

To my husband Ian, who has continued to support and understand my need to be close to Brian.

To my children Michael and Rebecca, two rare and wonderful people who are always there with their love and support. They make the effort to understand, and accept the signs Brian has given us. They chose to give me their love at a time in my life when I most needed it.

To Christine, who stood by me on good days and bad, giving me the hope and encouragement I needed.

To my good friends Margaret, Dorothy, Eileen, Elaine, and Trudy who have each helped me to understand the meaning of death and to realize the power of my faith. Thank you for listening when I cry, smiling when I laugh, and understanding as only another bereaved parent can.

To Carol who has done so much for me during the distressing years since this, the most tragic event of my life. You have lent a sensitive ear and helped me comprehend that I am not alone in my misery. Thank you, Carol, for your work with Compassionate Friends. It is because of your efforts that all bereaved parents in Kamloops have a place where they may go to share their grief.

To Father Michael who through his great wisdom has helped me understand my faith as I tried to make sense of my loss. Whose words of wisdom are forever etched in my heart and in my mind. You helped to renew my faith as I struggled down the path of fear and sorrow in search of answers.

To my family members, who have supported me and stood by me in ways I never would have believed possible. Thank you for letting me know that I am loved and accepted—faults and all! Especially I thank my parents, whose acceptance and encouragement is, as I have come at last to understand, unconditional; all I have to do is ask.

To my grandmothers, who taught me how to love and care for all children, and who made me the gift of their great wisdom and inner peace which I will carry with me, always.

To my "Al-Anon" friends, past and present: Thank you for being there.

To everyone who has helped me and encouraged me on my journey, including those such as Rosemary Aleta, and Oprah who will never know that they have helped me.

Many thanks to Varrie of Be Spoke Words for her editorial skills in fine-tuning this manuscript for publication. Without her encouragement, I may never have published this work.

My sincere gratitude and thanks to my dear friend Cristal Bowser of Cristal Clear Solutions who worked diligently editing my photos and designing the pages for this book.

I thank you all for being yourselves, and for bringing love and understanding into my life.

With love,

Kathy

Contents

Preface

Writing *With Love From Heaven* was difficult; revisiting the memories, receiving the signs, acknowledging that Brian will never be with me again—at least not in this lifetime as I know it. This thought hurts me deeply, but knowing that Brian has peace and happiness gives me some contentment. As I write, a passage from *Proud Spirit* by Rosemary Altea keeps entering my mind:

> Because I am love, and come from love, and because I am your teacher, I must tell you...if I could give you a gift for Christmas, I would give you the gift of pain...I would give you the gift of heartache...and I would give you the gift of tears...for it is only through these things that you will learn, that you will grow, and that you will come to understand the nature of your soul, and of your strength.

These words have given new strength to my life, and understanding to the loss of my son. Only now can I comprehend why Brian was in my life for so short a time. For it was Brian who taught me to love, laugh and cry; to forgive, pray and believe; and to accept unconditionally.

I truly believe Brian was and is an angel of God whose earthly purpose was to open my eyes to the kindness, sorrow, joy and beauty of this world. He has left me with overwhelming feelings of love and peace, and the tranquil acceptance of the world around me.

Brian in death, as in life, is lighting the way for me. I feel his presence each minute of every day. He has given me answers to questions I thought unanswerable, and brought me an inner contentment that I never thought possible.

The death of anyone close is difficult to bear, but the death of a child is the greatest loss many will ever endure. In **With Love From Heaven**, I tell of my many months of sorrow, grief and healing after Brian's death. There were also guilt, anger and feelings of isolation to be worked through. And there was learning anew how to accept life's trials and how to trust in God.

My journey has brought many wonderful and rare people into my life. I have also received numerous signs and read many books. All these elements united to help me find the strength to go on, to earn peace of mind, and to believe in life after death. For it is only through faith, prayer, love, and acceptance that we will find eternal happiness.

When he was eight years old, Brian said to me, "Mom, don't kill that fly! What did it ever do to you? He might have a family too, you know. Who will take care of them if you kill him?"

Now, whenever I think about swatting even the most annoying of flies I stop, remember Brian's kind, caring ways—and shoo the fly away. For Brian was right, even the smallest or most pesky insect has a purpose on earth.

When I see Brian's candlelight flickering each night, I always take time to say, "Hello, Brian. I miss you too." And the candle dances merrily in response.

When the physical body dies, people often say, "There was no cure, so he died." Or sometimes, "Too bad someone didn't find a way to help him. He might still be with us if they had."

However, I believe death is a cure. For in death the soul is released to continue its growth, free of pain and sorrow. Is this not the best cure of all?

Before Brian: The Mysterious Message

Though seasons change - Life is but a mystery

Before Brian:
The Mysterious Message

It was the summer of 1971 and I had just had my twenty-second birthday.

I was working in the dietary department of a local hospital for I was divorced with two small children to support. My son Michael was aged two-and-a-half and Rebecca, my baby, was only one year old. At this time in my life, the thought of ever having any more children was as far from my mind as eating liver. All I wanted to do was to be able to feed and clothe Michael and Rebecca. Times were tough but we had each other and that was what mattered most to me.

I had a friend, Anne, who worked with me at the hospital and who was much older than I was. Anne had only one child, an adopted daughter who had been in the same class as me at grade school. In those days, Anne was very lonely as she and her daughter had grown apart. Anne took an instant liking to my children and me and we spent many hours together outside the workplace.

Anne didn't drive often. She had high blood pressure so her doctor allowed her behind the wheel only on necessary trips—groceries, work, doctor's appointments, etc. One day she asked me, "Kathy, would you have time to drive me to see my fortuneteller?"

Anne used to visit her fortune teller, or psychic as we might now call her, on a regular basis, but she always had to rely on a friend for a ride since her estranged daughter no longer drove her. It so happened that my children were to visit an aunt that afternoon, so I answered, "Sure, Anne. I'd love to take you. In fact, it might be fun. I wonder if she'd tell my fortune, too, since I'll be there anyway?"

When Anne's consultation was finished, the fortuneteller came into her waiting room.

"I hear you would like your fortune today too!"

I replied hesitatingly—for all of a sudden I found my feet were getting very cold.

"Y-y-yes. I would, if it isn't too much trouble. If you're too busy, though, I could make it another day; I don't mind."

Just my luck—she had time! The psychic's house was spooky, and filled with shadows; I began to wonder what I had let myself into. As I entered her "ghost room" I grew ever more apprehensive. The room resembled a set for a horror movie. It was dirty, eerie and dimly lit; there was a kitchen table with cards on it; a parrot perched beside the table. I don't recall if there was a floor in the house or if it was just dirt. There were dirty cups and old discolored beads everywhere. And the parrot kept talking incoherently about things I knew nothing about in his jumbled language that only the fortuneteller could comprehend.

"Sit down and we'll get started"

I did as I was told, but I didn't dare move a muscle for fear that something would jump out and grab me—or that the parrot might decide to attack me! So…very fearfully, I watched the fortuneteller begin to examine the cards.

She told me many things which were true and accurate. She said I was recently divorced, had two children and came from a very large family. Then she told me all the usual things which I expected to hear. That I would meet a man and get married again in the near future; that, when I met this man, I would quit my job at the hospital to stay at home with my children; that there would be many changes in my life over the next few years and that I would soon be going on a trip. Finally she said, "Turn over three cards of your choice. They will be the cards of your destiny."

Quickly I turned over three cards. By now I was getting anxious to leave. I had had just about enough spookiness for one day. I thought, "Who believes in what fortunetellers say anyway? They are just a bunch of fakes making general statements about things that could happen to anyone—and then charging for their services. No one really believes this garbage." I knew I didn't take seriously what she said about my future.

That was before she looked at the three cards that I had turned over for her.

"Is your baby ill?" she asked quietly.

"No", I answered, thinking to myself, "Ah ha, she doesn't know what she is talking about!"

"The baby—it's not ill?" she asked. And her face became more grief-stricken as she looked at the next card.

Now I began to worry, but to my surprise, the psychic said abruptly, "I'm sorry, that will be all for today. I'm tired, so that will be all."

Rapidly I questioned her:

"What about the baby? What's wrong with the baby? Don't I get my three questions?"

For Anne had told me that, at the close of a consultation, the fortuneteller always granted the client three questions. But the psychic only motioned me to the door and repeated, "That will be all for today."

The last statement made by the fortuneteller began to gnaw at me. Perhaps because of her general accuracy in talking about my family, or maybe because of the signs of distress on her face, I could not dismiss her words from my mind. Silently, I repeated them over and over. And always I saw the look of horror and grief on the woman's face as she said, "That's all for today!"

After that visit, I kept a very close watch on my baby, Rebecca. I was always fearful something might happen to her. I became a nervous wreck!

The psychic's words remained fixed in my mind and on a spring day the following year, I offered to drive Anne to visit her fortuneteller, for I knew my friend still went on a regular basis for consultations. When Anne's turn was over, I inquired of the psychic, "Would you have time to tell my fortune today?"

"Yes, certainly," she replied.

It was obvious that the woman did not remember me from my earlier visit. For the second time in a year, I followed her into her dark, dreary room, but this time I had a purpose, to find out about my daughter's illness.

The fortuneteller went through her usual routine of statements about my past and present, and predictions about my future. Finally, as the session came to a close, she followed her usual procedure and invited me to pick three cards.

This time she did not say anything that worried or frightened me. The moment I had been waiting for came as she said, "Is there anything you would like to ask? You may have three questions."

"Yes," I said unhesitatingly.

"OK. I'm ready. Ask your first question."

The moment had come and I wasted no time as I queried, "The last time I was here you mentioned my baby. You asked if the baby was ill, then you put the cards away. I just want to know what you saw. Is something going to happen to my baby?"

The fortuneteller picked up a card and, as she looked at it, her face turned ashen. She looked up at me and quietly answered with sadness in her voice, "I must have been mistaken."

"But you said my baby was ill," I continued.

Again she spoke, softly, "I'm sorry. I don't remember. I must have made a mistake. I'm very tired now. These will be all the questions for today."

"Are you sure?" I demanded. "Please check again. I need to know what is going to happen to my baby."

She looked very solemn as she repeated, "I'm sorry. You'll have to go now. And just take good care of your baby. I'm sure everything will be just fine. I really must go lie down now. Good-bye."

I never did go back to see her, but for several years following that visit I worried that something terrible was going to happen to my baby daughter, Rebecca. Like a hawk, I watched her every move, never daring to let her out of my sight. I did everything for her—so much so, that when Christmas holidays came during her kindergarten year, her teacher came up to me and asked, "Can Rebecca dress herself?"

I replied, "Well, she's the baby and I sort of do everything for her. Usually I just sit her on my lap and dress her."

The teacher's next statement shocked me. "You have two weeks at home during Christmas with Rebecca. If she is to return to my class in January, she must be able to dress herself from head to toe—including ski suit, boots, and shoes! If she cannot do that, keep her home until next year when she is more capable of dressing herself. I have thirty other children in the room and I don't have time to baby-sit her."

After that, I stopped smothering Rebecca and started letting her live life more independently. After all, it had been nearly four years and she hadn't been sick even once during that time, except for the occasional cold.

When Michael was seven and Rebecca was six, I married again and we all moved to Canada. The incident with the fortuneteller had long been forgotten. And besides, our lives were looking up!

Now remarried, I desperately wanted another child. When Rebecca was two my gynecologist had told me that I was unable to have any more children but I was positive that they were wrong. I loved being a mother, and all I could think about was having another child. During that time it seemed everyone I met was either pregnant, or had a new baby. I had always planned to have all my children by the time I was thirty. I did not want to have children the same age as my grandchildren like my parents had. I wanted to be able to spoil my grandchildren as my grandparents had spoiled me. After two long years, I still did not have my baby, although I had experienced two miscarriages. Consequently, I prayed every night for another child.

A year and a half later, after another near-miscarriage and six months of bed rest, Brian Thomas was finally born on November 14, 1979. His brother, Michael, was now ten-and-a-half years old and his sister, Rebecca, was nine. Brian truly was a special gift from God. Doctors had already warned me that, if I lost Brian, another pregnancy would be too risky.

My doctor had stated, "Miscarriages are Nature's way of saying a baby has serious problems."

I didn't care. I had my new son. Medical problems were something I would deal with if and when the time came. At that moment my life was perfect.

Brian's Childhood: Surrounded by Angels

Brian's Childhood:
Surrounded by Angels

During his short life Brian was always surrounded by angels. Not only was he surrounded by angels, but all who met him said, "He's so beautiful; he looks like an angel."

And the truth was, Brian did look like an angel. He was perfect, and those statements about his appearance really frightened me. While I was growing up, I had often heard that children who looked like angels didn't live long. Angel children are here on earth for a purpose, and once that purpose is accomplished, they return to heaven.

Since childhood, I had associated the expression "Angel Child" with a poem by Edgar A. Guest. The title of the poem is *I'll Lend You for a Little Time* and it reads:

"I'll lend you for a little time a child of mine," He said.
"For you to love while he lives and mourn when he is dead.
It may be six or ten or twenty-two or three.
But will you till I call him back, take care of him for me?
He'll bring his charms to gladden you, and if his stay is brief
you'll have his lovely memories as solace for your grief.
I cannot promise he will stay, since all from earth return.
But there are lessons taught down there I want this child to learn.
I looked the wide world over in search for teachers true,
and from things that crowd life's lanes, I have chosen you.
Now will you give him all your love, not think the blessing vain,
nor hate me when I come to call, to take him home again."
For all the joys thy child shall bring, the risk of grief shall run.
We'll shelter him with tenderness, we'll love him while we may'

and for the happiness we've known, we'll ever grateful stay;
but should the angels call for him, much sooner than we planned,
we'll brave the bitter grief that comes and try to understand.

Isn't it ironic that this was the same poem we chose to have put on Brian's funeral cards so many years later? This simple little poem talks of the angels surrounding the life of a child. It suggests that the child was sent to earth to learn some lessons. We are reminded that when the child has completed his lessons, be it at an old age or at birth, he shall return to Heaven. The poem also describes the search for the right parents to love and shelter the child with tenderness while he is on earth. I was shown this poem by the funeral director when we were planning our son's funeral and I knew when we read it this was the only one for Brian. Rebecca and I, speaking at the same time, both said, "That's the one."

I first understood that Brian was surrounded by angels when, at the age of eighteen months, he had his first seizure. That first seizure, which happened in our car, left my infant son unconscious and blue-black in color. Somehow, somewhere within me, I rediscovered what I had been taught some eighteen years earlier in my eighth grade class on artificial respiration. I kept on praying to God to save my beautiful son, and from within came the knowledge that I needed to administer artificial respiration to my infant. Brian began to breathe again as his natural color returned. This was the first of many times when I had to administer artificial respiration to keep my son alive.

About twelve months later when he was approximately thirty months old, Brian entered what I refer to as a trance-like state. Until this time, the doctors that we consulted said that Brian's seizures were caused by fevers, and that he would eventually outgrow them. As we rushed him to Children's Hospital yet again, I wondered what would be next.

At Children's Hospital, I was told, after Brian had undergone several tests, that my imagination was overactive. I wanted to believe the doctors, but a voice within me said, "Don't listen. There is more to Brian's medical condition than has been discovered so far."

Although I trusted Brian's doctors, I told them we were unwilling to leave the hospital. I was fearful that something would happen to my son. I knew I had to listen to that unceasing inner voice and discover what came next.

The doctors conferred.

"There is one more test which we can do, if it would ease your mind. We more than likely won't find anything, but we'll give it our uppermost attention and hopefully set your mind at ease at the same time."

"We'll take it," I replied with relief in my voice. "I'm sure there is more to this child's medical condition than we have found out thus far, but I have the feeling we are nearer to an answer now. Thank you for listening to an 'overprotective' mother."

And so Brian was taken to another hospital for another type of brain scan, and what we hoped would be more concrete answers to his medical problems.

Thank goodness I did listen to that little voice within saying, "Don't leave the hospital. The doctors need to look more closely. Be persistent."

Because of my persistence and as a result of the brain scan taken at the General Hospital it was discovered that Brian had hydrocephalus, sometimes known as water on the brain. Now, the fluid which had accumulated in the brain of my son was not, as is usual in such cases, in a single mass. The doctors made a point of bringing me into the consulting room to look with them at Brian's scan results.

"We've never seen anything quite like it. Usually the fluid is in a mass, but Brian's is in the shape of a cross. We don't quite know what to make of it. We thought you might like to see it. From here on we will be monitoring your son on a regular basis to make sure the volume of fluid doesn't grow and the pressure on his brain doesn't increase.

This was only the beginning of Brian's long medical history. Brian had been a sickly child from the start with pneumonia at 6 months and numerous asthma attacks. At 18 months he started having seizures and later on going into mini trances. The older he grew, the more complicated life became. But it wasn't until he started having outbursts of unusual behavior patterns such as screaming and hanging onto his head, then not remembering why, that the doctors finally listened to me.

Soon we understood that Brian not only had several medical problems but also severe learning disabilities. The older Brian grew, the more noticeable the learning disabilities became. They set his life on a course marked by total disarray and unintentional mistakes. The older he got, the more he was teased and ridiculed by peers and adults alike. My beautiful son was headed down a troubled path, a path that no one could have predicted at the time of his first few visits to Children's Hospital.

The examining doctors seemed amazed that the fluid resting on my son's brain was in the shape of a cross. I, however, was not. I knew this was but another sign that Brian was surrounded by angels. I believed the voice that I had heard and continued to hear was just a warning from another angel about my son's medical problems, and a reminder to me not to give up, for the answer was so close. Now I knew for certain that Brian was special and that he had been sent to me for a purpose. I did not yet know what all this meant, but I did know that in God's time I would be given the answers. For now, prayer and listening to that inner voice were the important things. I was sure the answers would come to me in due time.

Brian's next encounter with one of his angels came when he was about five years old. She appeared in the most unusual of places—the parking lot of a grocery store and strip mall in New York State.

While the rest of the family remained in the car, Brian and I went quickly to pick up a few things for a trip to visit his grandparents in Hudson Falls. Brian was holding my hand as we walked across the busy parking lot. Suddenly Brian let go of my hand and darted towards the store. He had never done anything like this before. There was traffic coming from all directions. As Brian was about to dash across the main driveway, a car came towards him at a good speed. Panic-stricken, I tried to catch up with my son. My fear was so great that I was unable to get out a sound to alert him. In a split second, a speeding car and my son would collide!

From nowhere, a lady appeared across the driveway from us.

"Stop!" she screamed.

Brian instantly stopped and the car sped by, only inches from him.

At that moment I caught up with my son and grabbed his hand as I looked up to thank the lady who had saved him. There was no lady standing across the driveway from us. There was no lady in sight—anywhere.

I asked, "Brian, why did you let go of my hand and run like that?"

"I don't know," he answered.

We would learn later that Brian's unusual outbursts were due to pressure building up in his brain.

"I'm glad you listened when that lady yelled 'Stop!'"

Brian looked very confused as he replied, "I didn't hear any lady, I just stopped. When I looked up I saw that car."

All I knew for sure that day was that Brian had guardian angels looking out for him every step of his way. As I took my son's hand and crossed the driveway to the store, I whispered, "Thank you," to my inner self as much as to Brian's protector.

By the time Brian was five and a half, I was convinced that pressure was building up inside his skull. The incident in the parking lot, along with several other events, led me to that conclusion. So, once again I found myself seated beside Brian as he waited his turn to be examined by his doctor at Children's Hospital.

This visit to Doctor Montey's would prove to be one of the closest experiences with one of his angels that I can recall Brian having. We met the neurologist, Dr. Sterling, and the neurosurgeon, Dr. Montey, both of whom examined Brian, then left us in the examination room while they went to take another look at Brian's latest brain scans. Shortly after they went out, a dark-haired young man wearing a white lab-coat entered the room and closed the door behind him.

"Hi," he said. "I'm an intern. May I examine your son?"

He took from his pocket an instrument resembling a flashlight, similar to the one used by Brian's doctors. Using procedures identical to those used by the doctors who usually examined Brian, he looked into Brian's eyes with the aid of the light. After a few seconds he turned to me, "I know your son's problem," he said. "Ask for a milogram and you'll find the answers you need. Don't say who told you; you must say you read about it in a book. Don't mention me—but insist, and you'll find Brian's problem. Good luck!"

With that, the white-coated young man left. We never saw or heard from him again.

When Dr. Montey and Dr. Sterling returned to the examining room, no one mentioned an intern. I did as instructed and insisted on Brian's having a milogram. After much debate the doctors agreed. An appointment was made for Brian to have the milogram. This was the test that led the doctors to realize that Brian's spinal cord had been pinched from birth. An emergency Arnold Kharie operation was performed on Brian and for the time being all seemed to be well.

I did not see that intern again, but I shall never forget him. He was young, probably between twenty-five and twenty-eight years old, and he was tall with a slim build and dark hair. Swiftly he had gone about his business, and as quickly as he had entered the room—he had left. I knew he was one of Brian's guardian angels. I saw this angel up close and he looked just like any other intern at the hospital. In retrospect, the only thing which set him apart from the other doctors was that he did not turn off the room lights while examining Brian. The other doctors always turned off the lights before using a flashlight to look into Brian's eyes. I'm grateful to that angel for saving Brian's life that day, and I'm grateful he trusted me enough to let me see him. The appearance in the examination room of that intern was a testament to my faith—a faith I'm grateful to have and to hold on to.

Since that day, I've thanked God many times for sending a very special angel who saved my son. During his life on earth Brian was surrounded by many protecting angels. Like the lady and the intern, they showed themselves for only brief moments to help save my son. I know there were many more unseen angels working to keep him safe from harm and life's many challenges. We each have our special angels at our sides. All we have to do is ask for their help if we need it; they'll do what they can for us.

As I tucked Brian into bed one evening when he was about eight years old, he asked me a very disturbing question.

"Mom, what is it like to die? What does it feel like?"

"I don't know, Brian." I quickly responded. "I have never died. But, don't worry about it tonight; you're not going to die for a very long time."

I thought that would be the end of it but I was wrong. Brian continued, "But, Mom, I need to know. Is it cold there? Is it dark? Will I still be able to see you, Mom? Do you think it will hurt, Mom? What if I don't wake up again? What if I can never see you again, Mom? What will it be like there?"

"Don't worry, Brian," I repeated. "You aren't going to die for a very long time—way after Mommy and Daddy."

Brian persisted, "But what is it like there, Mom?"

I knew I had to answer him as best I could, so I told him, "I believe it's beautiful in Heaven. Everything is beautiful and perfect. When you die you, become one of God's angels. Now, go to sleep and don't worry about it; it's a long way off. Good night. Remember I love you."

That conversation with Brian still haunts me. Why would an eight-year-old boy worry so about death and dying? And why was he so uneasy about going to sleep and perhaps never waking up again?

I told Brian's doctors what he had said, and that I was apprehensive that he knew something I didn't.

"I'm concerned that Brian might know something or sense something that we don't know," I confessed. "Do you think that is possible? Does my son know something? Is he going to die in his sleep?"

The doctor tried to put my mind to rest. "He is just an eight-year-old boy with an overactive imagination. He's not going to die in his sleep, or any other way. He's just curious, that's all. Many children are fascinated with death. He'll get over it and move on to another big question tomorrow."

Brian never asked me again about death, but I did not forget our conversation on the subject, and I'm sure Brian didn't either. I can only assume I answered all his questions to his satisfaction, as he never again raised the subject. But for the rest of his growing up, I was sure Brian knew something I didn't understand.

I realize now that my son was trying to prepare me for his untimely death. At eighteen, Brian fell asleep and never woke up. It is my belief that at that moment, when he was eight, he remembered how he was going to die. I feel he had an urgent need to prepare me for that pending death. I think Brian also needed reassurance that where he was going after death was a beautiful place, and that he would still be with me. He wanted reassurance that I would never forget him; and how could I ever forget such a precious gift, my own son. I answered him then, as I believe today, that Brian is one of God's angels. It is beautiful where he is. He can see me and I can feel his presence. Brian is with me every minute of each day, and will be until it is my turn to join him in Heaven. I can only hope that as he passed from this world to the next, my words about beauty and angels comforted him and that he understood what I had been trying to tell him so many years earlier.

Many times, as I reflect on his life, I am awestruck by the level of understanding of life and love that Brian showed. As a young child, Brian understood the world at a level beyond his years. He loved all things. He was compassionate. If only he could have carried that understanding into his teens when cruel pressures overtook his strength and diminished his self-esteem. So many "if onlys"! But none can change what is written—not even a mother's dreams for her child's future.

Brian's troubled teenage years consumed his once-bright light, but still his angels were at his side. They watched; they waited; they stood ready to rescue him. I believe that, even when he turned towards drugs and alcohol, his angels were ever at his side, guiding us, helping to keep life together for Brian and me. Brian's experiences were all part of the plan to learn his predestined lessons.

When Brian was fifteen and had no school to attend, he was chosen from among the twelve applicants who applied to attend the Connection. Held in a special area in the local high school, the Connection was a trial program for learning disabled students who didn't respond well in the regular classroom. This program eventually proved to be a disaster for Brian, for the Connection was where he fell into the world of drug addiction. But it was outside its door that he met Christa, the one true love of his life. If it had not been for The Connection, he might never have experienced the sense of being needed, and the joy of taking care of another human being. He might never have had the opportunity to own his own home—if he had not met Christa.

When he was seventeen, we needed to give our son a fresh start in life. This new beginning resulted from a newspaper advertisement on behalf of a heli-logging school in British Columbia. I had never been one to read the newspaper regularly, but that day I did. And there it was—Brian's destiny. At the time when we needed funding assistance to send Brian to heli-logging school, a tip from the Adams Institute in Prince Albert, Saskatchewan pointed us in exactly the right direction at precisely the right time. Jointly, these miracles led to Brian being accepted by the heli-logging school and to his being funded by the Saskatchewan Learning Disabilities Association. Was it all coincidence? I believe Brian had angels on his side paving the way for him. There is an answer to every question. There is a reason for everything that happens. There is a path we each must follow to reach our final destination. We may not always understand why we must take a particular path but we must have faith in God and know that all things are for a reason. We are but students on a journey, gathering knowledge to bring with us to our final destination. The life process exposes us to love, fear, hurt, and joy; to sorrow, anger and happiness as we learn our lessons on earth. We chose our paths and our lessons before we ever came to earth to live them.

When Brian had to make a court appearance in British Columbia and I needed to be with him, yet another angel stepped in to help. We had less than one week to go and no means of getting there. Then I heard that inner voice saying "Air Miles", and again I paid heed to the voice. I knew it was too short notice to use Air Miles, nonetheless I telephoned. The Air Miles representative listened while I explained my desperate situation and then said, "Can you wait while I talk to my supervisor?"

I waited. Within minutes she had returned to the phone and was telling me that an exception had been made. Not only could she provide the plane tickets for my husband, Ian and me, but she could also arrange that we would have a rented car—and we would still have a few Air Miles left over.

Within the week we were flying towards Campbell River, British Columbia and I knew this was all made possible by my special son, and by his special connection with special beings—angels! Brian's angels, such as the lady who shouted "Stop!" and the young intern who told me to ask for a milogram, were usually very clear in their instructions. Both Brian and I had the good sense to listen to those angels and to follow their instructions without question.

When my son Brian's time was near, he did what I had most prayed for during the last two years of his life; he stopped using drugs. He also found work he enjoyed and was happy, two things I so wished for him. Always, these two goals had seemed to be just beyond his reach; now he had attained them. Even though the time left to him was short, he had reached a very important place in his life.

I recall Brian phoning me and announcing, "I quit drugs, Mom, just like I promised. And I'm doing what you sent me to school for, I've got a logging job in a real logging camp! I love it here, and it's beautiful. Mom, I always want to live in Kamloops and I can't wait until you move out here too! You'll love it here, Mom. I know you will."

For the first time in almost three years, my son was his former loving, happy self.

As I think back to the weeks just before Brian's death, I recall how Rebecca and I painted angels. In September 1998, ironically and without each other knowing it, both Rebecca and I took up the hobby of painting ceramic angels. Neither of us had painted ceramics since my daughter was nine years old and we went together to ceramics classes. I was painting an angel in natural coloring when my daughter visited me unexpectedly one day.

"Mom," she said, "I have the same angels that I'm painting at my house. I'm antiquing mine in gold, though."

October 1998

Sept. 1998

May 1998

Who decides who's to live & who's to die?

Oct. 1998

17

October 1998

When Brian phoned me three weeks later, on the evening of October 23 (I'll never forget that date), and gave me some rather strange instructions as he told me his thoughts on his future.

That last conversation I had with my youngest son went like this:

"Hello. Mom. I love my new job and the outdoors and earning my own money again. Mom, I need Dad to fax me my fire-suppression papers, the ones I got in heli-logging school. He needs to fax them to Vern at the logging camp where I'm working. I can't keep working without them, Mom, so please remind Dad. I need them faxed on Monday, October 26. It has to be Monday, so please don't let Dad forget, OK? If he can't get the fax to go through, tell him to call Vern at 3:00 p.m.; he will be in the house then. I love you, Mom. Oh, and Mom, just so you know, I'm never getting married and I'm never having kids. I just wanted you to know. I love you, Mom. Bye"

I tried to tell Brian that he would change his mind someday; he would meet a girl, settle down and even have children. Brian always wanted children and he had insisted that I save all his toys and clothes for them. "You'll change your mind and meet some nice girl and have children someday, Brian. Just give yourself time," I said.

But, Brian had little time left. Our conversation took place on Friday, October 23 and I did not hear from my son again. Usually, he phoned almost every day, but I thought he was waiting to tell me he had received the fire-suppression papers before he phoned on Monday.

At the time I recognized no warning, but after my son had died I remembered the unusual conversation and realized that, without knowing it, Brian was trying to prepare me for his death. On Monday at three o'clock, I reminded Ian to fax the papers to the logging camp. Since the fax wouldn't go through, Ian phoned Vern.

Vern just said, "You'd better phone the RCMP," then hung up.

Thinking Brian was back into drugs, Ian angrily phoned the RCMP. The words he heard that day still haunt both of us.

"Mr. Roberts, do you have a son named Brian?"

"Yes," answered Ian.

"Mr. Roberts, we hate to have to give you this information over the phone, but your son, Brian, is deceased. He was identified at the logging camp this morning. The young man who had the bunk above your son's found him sitting on the corner of his bed. Brian was already deceased. His body is at the morgue in Vernon where an autopsy is being performed. I'm sorry, Mr. Roberts. We saw no signs of foul play at the scene, though a thorough investigation is being done as a precautionary measure."

I had loved and protected my son for almost nineteen years, but nothing could have prepared me for his untimely death. Not his many messages to me of an early death; not the angels I was painting; not even my last conversation with my son. Brian died quietly on October 25, 1998. He died in his sleep, on a bottom bunk in a logging camp in Enderby, British Columbia.

On October 26, 1998, I got the worst message of my life

As I walked up the familiar Al-Anon steps, I heard the words, "Brian is dead"

"Brian who?" I asked, as I searched my memory for a member or husband named Brian from our group.

"Your Brian."

These words echoed over and over in my head as I desperately tried to grasp what was being said, to get out of this bad dream.

"Is this a joke?" I whispered. "I talked to Brian on Friday. He's fine. He's working in a logging camp; his dad faxed his papers today. Is this some kind of joke?"

I have a blurred memory of being taken home by friends.

We later learned through the coroner's report that our son had died of a seizure similar to those he had suffered in childhood. This final seizure, which caused his heart to stop, was not unlike the very first he had when he was eighteen months old. Brian had influenza at the time of his death, as did many of the young men at the logging camp; but he was the only one who died.

I am grateful to Brian for keeping his promise to me; the coroner's report showed no evidence of the use of drugs or alcohol at the time of his death. Our son was, as he had promised, substance-free and leading a good and rewarding life at the time of his passing. Brian's death devastated me, but through his many signs, he has also given me the strength to carry on. Now I start each day as if it were my last and I have learned to live life through the teachings of God. Brian's death has made me a much more spiritual person. Now I understand more about life and death, and I believe there is a life after death.

Our son is buried in Hillside Cemetery in Kamloops, British Columbia, the place where Brian told me he wanted to live forever.

Brian tried, without his conscious knowledge, to let me know that his time was near. He informed me he would never marry and would never have children, two things that he had wanted all his life. Moreover, the date of his death was clear in his unconscious mind for he told me the exact day and time that his dad should send the fax to the camp. Brian even knew that the fax machine would be turned off, so he gave me the phone number of the camp. I thought it unusual at the time when Brian gave me those last instructions that Vern would be inside, close to a telephone, at three o'clock in the afternoon, rather than at the logging site.

During our last conversation, Brian sounded content and very much at peace with himself. I always have felt cheated of the chance to say good-bye to my son, but in reality, I did have that chance. When Brian phoned me on that Friday, he was saying his final good-bye to me. I knew that at that moment his life was perfect for him.

No matter our age, be it three, eighteen or ninety, when our earthly mission is completed and we have learned what we must, then we shall return to heaven. None of us is exempt.

At Brian's funeral, one of the young girls present, a friend of his, came over to our family.

"I'm pregnant," she said, "and if I have a boy I'm going to name him after Brian. Brian was a good friend to us all, and he helped us see our true potential. He never put any of us down for any reason. When kids called me fat he would say, 'You're not fat; you look great just the way you are.' "

After meeting that girl, I kept repeating, "Pregnant. She's pregnant. Maybe she is having Brian's baby? Maybe there is a piece of him left for me to cling to?"

I later asked several of Brian's friends if the baby was his. I always received the same answer, and not the one that I prayed for.

"No. Brenda has a boyfriend, and he is her baby's father. She and Brian were only friends."

Then my daughter reminded me of Brian's words during my last conversation with him: "I'm never getting married and I'm never having kids."

Now I understood those words. Brian knew that his friend would be at his funeral. He knew that if I found out she was pregnant, I would want the child to be his. He had to warn me before I got hurt, and before I set my heart on the child being his. I was disappointed, but in the long run, I was grateful for Brian's last words to me. They may not have been the words I wanted to hear, but under the circumstances, they were the best words he could have given me.

I got yet another message from him on the day of Brian's funeral. I'm not sure how it came to me; it just did. As we were preparing to go to the church, a thought came into my head, and it came as a message of sorts. I turned to my mother and said, "You know, sometimes they bury people in the wrong spot, and they have to bury them again."

I don't know why I said that; it just came out.

"That's morbid," replied my mother, "Where did you ever hear that? That doesn't happen now. Let's just get to the church."

I remember thinking, "Sometimes it does happen. I just know." Then the thought was out of my head, and I was on my way to my son's funeral. The rest of the day went as planned and neither I nor anyone else thought any more about that statement.

On the Saturday morning following Brian's funeral I awoke early. I woke up my husband, telling him, "I have to go to the cemetery this morning."

"Not today; it's too soon," Ian replied as he looked at me. "But I'll take you there before you fly back with Becky."

"No!" I shouted. "I have to go this morning. I have to see Brian this morning."

Again Ian said, "It's too soon, Kathy. I'll take you in a day or so."

I got out of bed and began to dress, still insisting; "I have to go today, Ian. If you don't want to go, I'll go by myself, but I have to go today."

I had a desperate need to see Brian right away.

Ian got up, dressed, and ate. Then he said, "If you really want to go that badly, I'll take you. But I do think it is too soon."

At that moment, I was ready. I had to follow my heart and go to Brian right away—even if I didn't understand why.

As soon as I got out of the car at the cemetery, I knew why I was there. I took one look at my son's gravesite and sobbed, "Brian is buried in the wrong spot. There isn't room for three graves in this area. We asked for three spaces so that we could be buried next to him, and there isn't room."

I looked puzzled as Ian tried to console me, "There's room. They just squish the caskets close together; but there's plenty of room for three. Now, I'd better take you home."

"Ian, this is the wrong spot," I insisted. "And they don't squish the caskets together. They buried Brian in a single space. I have to be buried next to him. They made a mistake!"

More to humour me than for any other reason, Ian whispered, "Will it make you feel any better if I phone the funeral parlor and relay your concerns to them?"

I nodded my head. "Yes."

Minutes later, Ian was on his car phone, dialing the number of the funeral parlor. I heard Ian ask, "Could there be a mistake in Brian's burial spot? My wife seems to feel that there isn't enough space for three caskets where Brian is buried."

Without hesitating, the funeral director replied, "Your wife is right. I forgot your request for three plots and had Brian placed in a single gravesite. I'm sorry. It's my fault. We'll correct the situation, but it won't be until Monday because the city workers are off for the weekend. But they will exhume his coffin on Monday afternoon and we will rebury him on Tuesday morning for you. I'm really sorry for the mistake, Mr. Roberts."

Now I knew why that thought came into my head on the morning of the funeral. It had been a message from Brian about the cemetery plot. Brian knew what my wishes were and he did not want the mistake to go unnoticed.

The premonition about the gravesite was but the first of a series of messages Brian would send me over the next year. All Brian's messages came to me with love, from Heaven. Even though I knew that Brian in the physical form that I had known was gone, I also learned that through spirit, love and thought Brian was with me and always would be with me. We are still very close and I talk to him daily. Sometimes he responds; sometimes he just listens; but he is always there to protect me and give me strength when I most need his encouragement and help.

While we waited for the funeral director to complete preparations for the reburial, Father Michael gave Ian and me information which I will always cherish. The information that confirmed what I had always known. My interpretation of what Father Michael told us that day is that death is just another dimension and our loved ones can reach us when they need to; and they do send us messages. All we have to do is listen and we will hear them.

First Father Michael asked, "Was your son concerned about the earth and the world around him?"

"Yes," I answered without hesitation. "Brian was concerned about everything and everybody—from the tallest tree to the smallest ant, and everything in between. He was also a child deeply interested in the welfare of all humans, especially those challenged or less fortunate. Brian always felt that all people should be equal on this earth. Why do you ask, Father?"

"I spent lots of time in the church with your son over the last few days that his casket was there. We got to know each other fairly well, Brian and I." Father Michael continued by saying something I will remember throughout eternity.

"Your son came and sat at the foot of my bed last night; I recognized him because I spent so much time with him in church. Brian said to me, 'Sir, I was just wondering why you put all those metal boxes into the ground? They only ruin the earth, you know.' Then Brian was gone; but I knew it was him," Father Michael continued. "That was why I asked you about your son's concern about the earth."

I was very grateful to Father Michael for sharing this experience with me. His words made me absolutely certain that I was right. Now I was sure that there is a life after death and that we can communicate with our loved ones, if only we truly believe, and listen closely enough to hear their messages. My son had sent me a sign that he had made it to Heaven. Brian knew I would listen to Father Michael. He knew I would recognize his kind, caring ways in Father Michael's report of the conversation with him. From that moment on, I knew that my Brian was well, would always be with me, and would always be my son.

The circumstances around Brian's re-interment and my conversation with Father Michael started me thinking about what happens after physical death and led, ultimately, to my writing this book. I now needed to know the answers to those questions which Brian had asked me so many years before. Where is Heaven? Where do we go after death, and what does it look like when we get there? I already knew from church that Heaven is a beautiful, peaceful place but now I needed to know more. I became ever more determined to learn all I could about death, dying, Heaven, eternity, and life after death. I found that I needed to think, read and learn a lot about life after death in order to be able to cope with the loss of my son. I needed to understand why he had to leave when he was so young, especially since he had turned his life around and was doing so well.

I knew I had my faith, and my strong belief in the teachings of the Catholic Church, but for me there still remained unanswered questions. And so began my journey of love and sorrow, my mission to learn about and understand this state we call death.

The beginning of my journey was haunted by losses sustained by both my grandmothers. Grandmother Crandall lost a baby, Winfield, when he was an infant. A picture of him hung on the wall, but he was never spoken of. I felt he should have been.

My Grandmother Kill's daughter, Catherine, died at the age of two. Likewise, her photograph hung on the wall and, although I knew I was named after her, I knew little else. I didn't want Brian's memory, his smile, or his life to be forgotten. I intended my grandchildren should know their uncle as a person—not merely as a picture on a wall.

Then I recalled the death of my Uncle Clyde at thirty-two. He had been my godfather, and when I was twelve, he died. I remember being at Uncle Clyde's funeral and seeing Grandmother Kill cry so much, and hearing her say how young he was. As a child I didn't realize how young my uncle had been at the time of his death, all I kept thinking was how sad everybody was. And after his funeral, Uncle Clyde was never again mentioned. Oh yes, his picture hung on the wall, but no one talked about him, or his life, or their memories of him.

One day I visited my grandmother by myself. "Gram, can I have something of Uncle Clyde's?" I asked.

"Come with me," she whispered, "and don't mention this to anyone."

We went upstairs to a room which was always kept locked. Gram unlocked the door, revealing what I took to be a large room filled with old junk. Then she opened a musty-smelling, wooden trunk and took from it a white cotton shirt and a pair of green marble cufflinks. These had belonged to my godfather, and Gram gave them to me saying, "Take good care of these and don't mention it to anyone."

I was grateful for the mementos but I always wondered why her dead children were never spoken of. To me, Grandmother Kill always seemed so happy, almost as if she had forgotten Catherine and Clyde. Now I try to understand. In the company of the bereaved, some people feel uncomfortable talking about loss and death, as if these experiences might be contagious. Others try to go on with daily living as if nothing distressing has happened. I was determined that no one who had known him should ever forget my son, their grandchild, their brother...uncle...nephew...friend. I would never hide his belongings or put away his pictures, and I intended to talk about this son of mine to all who would listen.

November 1998: Reality Takes Hold

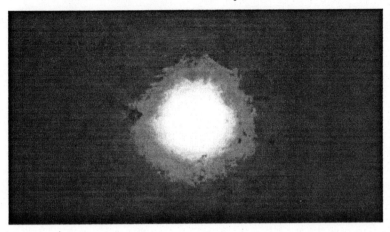

Despiration, guilt, loneliness - will it ever end?

November 1998:
Reality Takes Hold

For now, I had to return to Prince Albert, without Ian. As I walked with Becky and my infant grandson Joshua onto the tarmac at Kamloops airport, I did not know how I would be able to survive the death of Brian. Becky and I were both very, very quiet on the flight back to Prince Albert, each absorbed in our own thoughts.

During the flight as I gazed out at the endless sky of clear blue, an overwhelming peace and sense of well-being came over me. I knew that I would survive this, and that Brian would be with me now and always. As I searched the sky, I couldn't see him, but I knew he was there. I could feel Brian's presence and his joy and contentment—contentment which he was never privileged to experience while on earth. I knew my life was going to be different—harder. But I knew also that I would survive and my life would go on—it would have a new meaning, but it would go on.

I returned to Prince Albert from Kamloops where I had buried my youngest son, Brian. But the upsets in our lives were not over. Ian was still in Kamloops but planned to follow me to Prince Albert in one week. In the meantime, I had to close my daycare service, prepare to sell our home; the home where we hard raised our youngest child, and plan a memorial service for Brian so that his friends in Prince Albert would also be able to say goodbye.

There was so much to be done and I felt very alone. I should have moved to Kamloops when Ian and Brian wanted me to; but I had been so independent and so strong-willed and had insisted that I would move in my own time. Now it was too late for spending time with Brian; too late for him to show me the beauty he found in Kamloops. The "what ifs" were already besieging my mind and I had not yet unlocked the front door.

I returned to work at my daycare on the Wednesday following my son's burial. I was numb. I could not face anyone. For the next two weeks life was a blur. I felt my life was over, and that I should have been buried with Brian. I did not want to meet the parents who came to the daycare; I did not wish to answer their questions. I made myself scarce. My assistant greeted all the parents in the morning, and Becky met them in the evening to tell them about how the day had gone for each child.

This was truly a terrible time for me, besides arranging a memorial service for Brian and closing my business, I had to say goodbye to all the children I had cared for during the past two years. I also had to say goodbye to my many friends, but the hardest good-byes would be to my best friend—my daughter Rebecca, and to my two sweet grandsons.

As a parent, I felt that I had failed my son, for he was dead. I was the one who was supposed to protect him, but I hadn't done my job. How could I expect to be able to care for another person's child if I was unsuccessful in caring for and protecting my own son? At that moment, I decided that I would never again take care of children professionally. I wanted only to be a loving mother and grandmother and nothing more.

Repeatedly I asked myself, "What could I have done differently? Did I miss signs that Brian was ill?" My mind raced with "what ifs" and "if onlys". I prayed that this was all a bad dream. I wanted Brian, with his big brown eyes and his beautiful smile, to walk through the doorway and say, "I'm here, Mom. Don't worry—it's cool."

But another part of me was crying, "Get real, Kathy. Your son is dead. He will not be coming home, ever again. He'll never again smile at you, or hug you, or tell you that he loves you. Never again will you touch his hand, get him out of scrapes, or respond to his phone calls and to his cries for help. He is gone.

Again and again, that cold and final word rang in my head. Dead! I wanted to cover my ears and scream, "Stop!" but I couldn't get the word out.

I had to shake myself out of this state. I had children to look after—other people's children. I must concentrate on them for they were my responsibility until I could make other arrangements for their care on behalf of their families. One thing I did know was that these little children would be good for me right now. They loved me unconditionally and I knew their smiles. But they were not mine, and I was planning to close the daycare and move away, to be with my husband and Brian. I promised myself that I would never leave Brian again. The children I cared for professionally didn't understand my grief. They knew only that auntie had been away and was back again. They hugged me and kissed me, and did not judge me responsible for the loss of my son as I feared their parents might. It was much later that I found out that, of course, the parents of my daycare charges did not condemn me. They wished only to console me.

Finally, after two weeks of searching for a suitable replacement who would give the same energy and love to my daycare children as I had given, it was decided that, until the end of December, Rebecca would leave her work as a substitute teacher. She would look after the children until their parents could make alternative arrangements. As of Friday, November 12, 1998, I would no longer care for children.

The parents of all my daycare charges seemed to be very understanding and sent me their best wishes for my future. Only one parent was irate. Also, each one of them wrote recommending me highly. Several members, both parents and board officers, of the co-operative daycare which I had managed before opening my own daycare also sent me letters of recommendation, besides sending me letters expressing their sympathy for my loss.

In September 1998, Ian had moved to Kamloops to live in our new home, work and commute to Prince Albert. He drove back to Prince Albert from British Columbia to be with me until after Brian's memorial service on November 14. I found the memorial service so final. Brian's death was now permanent.

Brian's memorial service was held on the day that should have been his nineteenth birthday. He had so looked forward to this birthday! He couldn't wait to celebrate with his friends, because, after all he had been through, he had made it to his legal majority. He was drug and alcohol free, and he had a real job. He often reminded me that he had spent his eighteenth birthday in juvenile custody. He was ready to celebrate his success in life, and his personal freedom. Instead of a party to mark his birthday, there would be a memorial service to celebrate his life. But I knew I'd get through and that Brian would be watching, and saying, "Thanks, Mom. It's great."

The first thing that I did when I arrived back to Prince Albert was to phone my friend Michele, who makes stepping stones in stained glass. I asked her to design and create a stepping stone bearing an angel and Brian' name. There was an exceptional urgency in this commission for I needed the stepping stone for Brian's memorial service to be held in just a little more than one week's time. Michele said she could complete the stone by then, and she did.

The stepping stone added beauty and significance. I knew Brian would love it. On the day of the memorial service, I placed it in St Joseph's Church along with flowers from his friends and photographs of him as an infant and as a teenager. Also on the table, enclosed in a single frame, was a professionally mounted photograph showing Brian in death and one of his funeral cards. The memorial table for Brian added serenity to the moment. Old friends and neighbours rose to talk about the Brian they knew and loved. After the service, I gave Ian the stepping-stone to take back to Kamloops.

"Will you please put this on Brian's grave until his headstone is ready in the spring?" I asked. "I never again want to not know where my son is."

And Ian put the stepping stone on Brian's grave, where it stayed until spring, when the headstone was put in place. The angel stepping-stone is now a permanent part of the beautiful garden I have made behind our house in memory of my very special son.

From the blur of the memorial service, I recognize some of my Beta Sigma Phi sisters; I remember seeing Olive, my friend and neighbour, and there was Pat Graham who had always been very fond of Brian. My friends from Al-Anon were present and I saw Christine, my life-saving friend, but the other faces are now a blur. I was so confused that I whispered to Rebecca, "Do you know who that woman is?"—I did not recognize my friend Marion!

There were representatives present from the company that Ian worked for, and I remember telling one of them, "My Brian was a good kid. All he ever wanted was to follow in his father's footsteps."

I just needed them to understand my son. When Brian had worked for G & M, I was told that there was no room for mistakes in their business. I wanted them to realize that Brian may have had learning disabilities, but he was a good person. And he was certainly not a mistake in my life!

I recall that later in the service people from the Connection brought flowers. I remembered talking to Jenny and Mike, who were business associates of Ian's and who had known Brian quite well. Jenny reminisced about being Brian's swimming instructor and about what a fish he had been.

"Actually, he was more like a catfish, always preferring to swim on the bottom of the pool."

I knew the family of my son-in-law, Alain, were there and I recall seeing, out of the corner of my eye, my little grandson, Taylor. He was crying below the altar.

"Is Taylor OK?" I asked and I learned later that he was crying because he saw me crying, and thought I was hurt.

There were Brian's friends and Christa, his former girlfriend. How I wished I had encouraged her to stay out in British Columbia with Brian—or even encouraged them to have a child. How I now longed for just a little piece of Brian to remain with us! But I knew there would be no new boughs on our family tree nor heirs to carry on the Roberts name. Brian was gone, now. Oh how I wished! But deep down I knew it was for the best that no little child suffer the loss of his or her dad, and no young woman be left to raise a child, alone.

Then I spotted Eileen in the procession. Eileen was more than a long-time friend for she had also worked for me for many years. She had cared greatly for Brian, whom she always called "the little imp". We both hugged each other for a long time.

Eileen whispered, "I really loved that kid, you know; even if he was a little shit, I still loved him."

Well, the memorial service was over and I had survived the day, and I knew I would survive many more, whether I wanted to or not.

There remained two more duties to complete, then I could move to Kamloops and be with Ian. Move to Kamloops! Hadn't I balked at moving to Kamloops for those many months when my son was alive? Months when he had begged me to move, but when I wouldn't close my daycare and give up my nearby friends and grandchildren to be with my youngest son. Now I would move to Kamloops with Ian, but without Brian to care for. But Brian was in Kamloops where he had wanted to live forever. Now this beautiful city would hold his earthly body while his spirit body is forever in the beauty of Heaven. All I could think of was that deep, cold hole at Hillside Cemetery where Brian's body rested, surrounded by things he had loved: pictures of his family; letters and mementos from his friends; and wearing his favorite brand of clothes—"Tommy Hilfiger". When it is our time, Ian and I will join him. But first I had to close my daycare business.

The other task which I had to complete before moving was to set up a jewelry kiosk for a man in Florida and run it for him. The kiosk was due to open on November 14, Brian's memorial day. I had promised to run the kiosk for him for one more Christmas season and it was now too late to back out of the commitment.

"You must stand by your word and do as you promised," said Ian. "Open the kiosk."

I decided not to hire anyone this year and to run the kiosk myself. I felt that being occupied might keep my mind off my loss while I waited for Ian to return to Prince Albert to move me to Kamloops.

That which only a month ago had promised to be an enjoyable six weeks now seemed an overpowering nightmare. But maybe it would be good therapy for me to have the kiosk to focus on while waiting to move to Kamloops. I kept thinking how strange life is, for it continues—with or without the ones you love. Part of me felt that my life had come to an abrupt end, yet here I was at a congested shopping mall, setting up a business for a man I had never met. All those people bustling by. Busy people…laughing, shopping, and enjoying a family outing.

I wanted to scream at them, "What's so funny? Why are you here? Why are you all laughing? Don't any of you realize I just buried one of my sons? Do you remember Brian, the one you laughed at and teased at school? That wonderful young man I called Son? Don't any of you understand that today was to have been his nineteenth birthday, a day he couldn't wait to celebrate? Does no one care?

As I looked through teary eyes I asked myself, "What's wrong with people today?" I could not understand the world in which I lived. At the close of Brian's memorial service people had simply left, gone about their usual business, and continued with their lives. But my life had been changed completely.

On November 15, I immersed myself in the work of running the jewelry kiosk. I worked eighty-two hours each week until I closed the kiosk on December 30. Ian returned to British Columbia. Now I had only my work at the jewelry kiosk. With the help of Christine and my other friends, I managed to make it through each day. I remember little of what I did during these six last weeks of 1998. Repeatedly, I found myself lured into the pain of reliving and re-examining. If it had not been for Christine and Louise, I may not have been able to cope.

Thank goodness for my friend Louise! Daily she would visit me at work to find out if I needed anything; sometimes she would bring me lunch. And what would I have done without Christine, another dear friend? Christine is a strong person and she became a lifeline for me during this lonely time. She continues to support me each day as I write this book. Christine saw that I needed something to keep my brain working and occupy my attention in between sales of jewelry items. She brought me three tablets of lined paper and a pen.

"Kathy, you always said that one day you were going to write the story of Brian's life. Now is the time to get started. You write and I'll type," she stated with gentle firmness. I'm sure Christine suggested the project only because, at the time, she believed it would help me to heal. Little did she know what she was in for! Once I had started writing, I could not stop. Sometimes putting Brian's story on paper was easy; sometimes I wept; but always Christine was there to lend an ear. She helped me to understand, to learn, and to come to grips with my loss.

Zombie-like, I completed my daily round. Thank goodness for my daughter, my son-in-law and my grandchildren, for it was they who brought light, pleasure and joy into my life. I so looked forward to those days when they would visit me at the sparkling kiosk in the mall. My grandchildren were the sunshine in a very gray life.

And thank goodness for Ian and for telephones. Each night he lifted my spirits from afar. Then, too, I had my photos, my memories, and my dreams where I could take refuge from the painful reality of each lonely minute.

During the lonely evenings at my home in Prince Albert, I made Brian a Christmas present. I made an angel for him. Becky brought flowers from her wedding dress and put them in the angel's clasped hands. I found the ideal picture frame, cut out a photograph of Brian taken at a very happy moment in his life and glued it on a picture of the ocean, which was his favorite place. I put the framed photo with the angel and wrote on the frame, "Merry Christmas, Brian. We miss you and love you lots. XX00 Mom and Dad."

Ian took it all back to Kamloops, where he built a bench for the angel to sit on. He then added some artificial snow and finally made a glass case to enclose the gift. The men at Ian's Kamloops office made a stand, and Ian placed our gift to Brian at the cemetery. We put, and will continue to put that Christmas Angel at Hillside Cemetery each Christmas season for our son. I know he loves it.

So this is Christmas?

I don't want Christmas to come.

Why can't I be left
alone like this angel,
to just sit in silent
memory of my son,
who is here no more.

So This Is Christmas?

Christmas was approaching, and for the first time in my life, I didn't care if it came or not. The thought of Christmas without Brian to brighten the day was devastating to me.

I just didn't get it. How could life be this cruel to me? Many times the days and nights ran together. I lived as an automaton would; I was dead inside. I did only what was expected of me. I, who had always loved life, now saw nothing but the eternity I must wade through until I was called to join my son.

As I worked each day at the kiosk, I would ask myself, "Why are the stores decorated? Why do they continuously play these silly Christmas songs? Where is everyone going in such a big hurry, and why does no one notice me here alone, and very lonely?"

I saw the smiles on the faces of passers-by as they bustled through the stores with their packages and children in tow. Santa had been put right next to my kiosk, and many stopped to visit him and to be given a candy cane, and to have a photograph taken. I thought how commercialized and foolish this occasion they call Christmas had become. I was no longer one of the bustling passers-by. I did not want to celebrate Christmas ever again. I wanted to skip the whole thing—to go from October 1 to January 31 without ever wakening up.

Ian asked, "What do you want for Christmas this year?" Any other year, I would have had a list a mile long of things I wanted. Wanted, but did not need, for the truth was I did not really need anything.

"I don't even want Christmas to come," I answered blankly. "I don't want anything you can buy me. If you really want to know, I want Brian back here beside me; that's what I want. Can you buy that for me?"

Ian was sad and angry most of the time. He didn't know what to do to make me happy, to help me towards happiness. He didn't know how to relieve my hurt and sadness. He couldn't buy me happiness. He could do nothing other than be there, watch, and wait for me to come to terms with my life as it now was, without Brian.

I was angry or sad every minute of the day. I used to be like a little kid in a candy store when Christmas came, but not this year. This year I hated Christmas and all its commercialization. But wasn't it only last year when I couldn't wait to get to the stores to purchase just the right gift for each person on my list? Wasn't I the one who overbought for the kids and the grandchildren? This year it was a chore even to think about what I should give them. All I could remember was how much Brian had loved Christmas. How excited he would be for months before! He would give me lists, try to find my hiding places, and help me with the decorations. This year we weren't even having a tree—and certainly not decorations. I remembered how excited Brian had been in May, and even right through until October, as he told me that this year he was coming home to spend Christmas with me. Excitedly, we made our plans for the holiday season, for Brian had spent Christmas 1997 in youth custody and had been able only to talk to me on the phone.

But a cruel trick had been played. Brian was supposed to be with us, happily opening all the great gifts I should have selected for him. Instead, he was gone. I wondered if I would ever again love life as I once did. They say time heals all wounds, and I hoped my wound would hurt less as months went by, but I knew it would never heal.

I could only think upon things that would never be again. We would never again decorate the Christmas tree together. Never again would I fill the special stocking with Brian's name on it. There would be no more scavenger hunts for the coveted "big gift."

I was able to buy one or two small gifts for Ian. I needed him to know that I still loved him and, goodness knows I wasn't showering him with affection these days—only tears and anger. I was also able to choose presents for my children and grandchildren. My misery wasn't their fault, and I knew they too must have been hurting. But all was done robotically; there was no longer any joy attached to the season I had once loved.

At Rebecca's insistence, Ian and I spent Christmas Day at her home. My daughter served a superb meal in her beautifully decorated home and her choice of gifts was perfect. She did all the things that I used to be responsible for. Why was it that she had to take over as head of the household years before she should have? And why did her duties always seem to revolve around her younger brother? Rebecca, ever mature beyond her years and always there to take control over a difficult situation in my absence: first, when her brother had been ill so many years ago; and now, after his death. What would my life have been like without her?

I was so grateful for the way Rebecca and Alain helped us through Christmas Day. They talked about Brian. We laughed at the funny things he had done, and we discussed the sad times, even speaking about his addictions. Together, we remembered him.

Since childhood, Rebecca's mature attitude had meant that she could always take over some of my responsibilities at a minute's notice. Many times she seemed to know what I needed even before I myself knew. Thank goodness for my daughter, and for my wonderful son-in-law. Alain is one of the kindest men I know, and in many ways is a lot like Ian.

I received a very special Christmas gift from Rebecca and her husband. It was truly a gift from the heart and will remain one of my most cherished possessions. Together, my daughter and son-in-law made for me a country church, complete with stained-glass windows, wooden pews, golden chalice, and even a Bible on the altar. I had mentioned in the summer that I wished Alain could make me a little church some day. Never in my wildest dreams did I think he would have the time to do this; but there it was, in all its perfection. It is one of the most beautiful things I have in my home. The little-big church sure brightened my Christmas Day and it made me realize how lucky I was. It reminded me to count my blessings instead of my misfortunes.

And now there was Michael at my side, my eldest son who was always so quiet and who asked so little from me. If anything good came from the loss of Brian, it had to be the closeness Mike and I found. Before, he had always been in the shadow of his younger sister and baby brother, now he took the initiative. Now he phoned me often; he talked to me about Brian. When I most needed him, Michael was there. He even spoke to me about moving to Kamloops to live at some time in the future. This was what I would have loved, to have my two surviving children and all my grandchildren living right next door to me. I never again wanted to be away from my children. But that was make-believe. The reality was that in a few days I would leave behind me the life I had known and move three thousand miles across the country.

Brian's death also brought my parents and me closer to each other. We had been estranged for several years. I was very cautious about getting too close lest I be hurt. Now I enjoyed the warm feeling of getting to know them all over again. Tragedy may either tear a family apart, or pull it together. We were being pulled together, thank goodness and I believe that Brian was behind this. Some of his last conversations were about how he wanted to get to know his family—the grandparents, aunts, uncles and cousin whom, for the most part, he hardly knew. I knew Brian would have wanted us to become closer. He had always been the kind, gentle child trying to make peace in the world, and where better to begin than at home?

It was a very sad season for me. Not only were there no tree, no stockings and no decorations, but I would be moving to an unfamiliar province right after Christmas. I would be leaving behind my daughter, my grandchildren, and my supportive friends.

Christmas 1998 was filled with gloom, and was so very lonely, for I knew I was leaving behind all that was dear to me. Ian and I were supposed to be excited about starting a new life in a beautiful city, where the climate was not so harsh and our home looked onto mountains and the river. But to me the move seemed more like a sentence of death, for I was going to a city which held for me only one memory, that of my son's funeral.

It was then that I started talking to Brian each day. I asked him to give me strength and to be always by my side. Without knowing it, I was beginning to learn about life after death, about dying, and about faith. I started thanking God each day for the gift of Brian in my life and for our shared time on earth. It is my belief that God extended Brian's life beyond that first seizure, beyond the near-accident in the parking lot and the meeting with the angel who understood Brian's medical condition, because He felt I had so much to learn from this child. The death of my youngest son taught me much about my own life, about the world I lived in, and about the meaning of love.

Christmas came and went. The household goods were packed now, except for our bed and a few personal things. I was still afraid to move away from Rebecca and the boys and the town where we had raised Brian. Even leaving behind his room was hateful to me. Brian had never lived in the new house in Kamloops; he had no presence there. But I knew I had to leave Prince Albert, for my husband was getting tired of commuting between British Columbia and Saskatchewan. Brian's death had taken its toll on Ian too. His work was suffering and his company had been very patient. Now it was time for me to be fair to him. We needed each other as never before.

The last thing I did before leaving my former life in Prince Albert was to purchase a little guardian-angel pin set with Brian's birthstone. I now knew that Brian would always be at my side, wherever I might travel or live. I always wear my guardian angel, for it makes me feel closer to my beloved Brian, and reminds me that he is only a thought away.

As we loaded our four dogs into the car and locked the front door of what had been our home, I was filled with certainty that I would never again live in Prince

Albert. I knew for certain that I would never leave the city where my youngest child was now laid to rest.

We were both silent as we began the eighteen-hour drive. As we got closer to Kamloops, I knew that it would be the city where I would belong and where I would live from now on. There seemed to be a far away voice whispering in my ear, "You won't regret the move. It's your destiny, the place where you are meant to be. One day you shall understand, but for now you must just believe and follow your thoughts." Why had I not moved there when my younger son had begged me to? Why had I waited so long?

1999 Begins

I got to work editing my book
"Brian's World" ... Brian's friend Amber
kept me company as often as possible.

1999 Begins

Through snowstorm and blizzard we drove, but eighteen hours later, on what was New Years Eve, we arrived safely in Kamloops. Our house was only partially furnished as Ian had been "making do" since September with the minimum, essential furnishings he had brought with him in the fall. All Brian's furniture was still stored in the garage. Ian had collected it from Brian's apartment shortly after our son's death and there it sat, a chilling reminder.

As I sadly looked at the forlorn pile, Ian admitted, "I didn't know where you wanted his things, so I just left them here." I stood, stared and remembered. There was Brian's bedroom set he had worked so hard to pay for and which he had loved so much. There were his books, his pictures and his bicycle helmet. These things were all just sitting there staring back at me, but their young owner was gone. These things that we had so taken for granted had been a part of my younger son; they were precious to me and I knew I would never be able to part with them.

Finally, Ian's words came through the stillness of the moment.

"What do you want to do with all this stuff?"

"I want to take one of the bedrooms upstairs and use it for Brian. I want to put his room back together for him the way it used to be in our Prince Albert home. I want Brian to have a place in our house to call his own. I want him to always feel welcome here. I need to know that there is still a room for Brian. I need him to know that he is still a part of our life and that he is welcome here any time. I never want to forget our son. I want our grandchildren to know their Uncle Brian too."

Our household furnishings arrived on January 3, 1999. There was much to do and a lot to unpack. We opened boxes as they were brought into the house and placed their contents wherever we could find room. We had moved to a smaller house and, as well as our personal effects, I still had all my daycare equipment. But for now, I was most interested in the boxes containing Brian's clothes, toys, trophies and collections. I had a need to arrange his room first. The rest of the house could wait until I had time.

From the first minute I stepped into our new home, I begged Brian to contact me. I needed to hear from him, to know he was OK. I needed a sign, something to let me know he was with me.

During the second night I spent in our new home, I awoke to the sound of music and talking. The sounds I heard were not coming from inside our room; they were more distant than that, but I could hear them. I knew the noise wasn't coming from any of the neighboring homes for they were too far away. I woke up Ian, and he too heard the sounds. This happened several nights in succession until one night Ian got up and began to search for the source of the noise. When he went down to the kitchen, he found that an old radio sitting on the counter was turned on. He turned it off and came back to bed.

On each of the next twelve nights, the radio came on at about 2 a.m. and each night I woke up Ian so that he too would hear it. I knew the music from the radio was a sign from Brian. I knew he was only answering my request to let me know he was doing fine. He wanted me to know that he was watching over me and that he was safe. At the end of the second week of being wakened each night by noise from the radio, I told Ian my belief about the radio's message. That morning Ian put the radio in the garbage bin, all the while mumbling about either the radio being broken, or someone having set its timer by mistake. I checked the radio. It was not switched on and neither had the timer been set. But I think Ian was nervous when I told him it was Brian's way of communicating with me. I think my husband may have believed that I was losing my mind. It was not until several months later that Ian came to believe what I already knew—that there is life after death.

We began to worship at Holy Family Church immediately after arriving in Kamloops. It is a bit smaller than the church we attended in Prince Albert but, besides being in our neighborhood, this was the church which held bittersweet memories of our son's funeral mass and I could not consider worshiping elsewhere. I consoled myself by thinking that maybe there was a reason why I had been led to this church in the first place. I knew the people were friendly and I both greatly respected and felt at ease with Father Michael. I knew he understood my loss and I felt he knew as I did that there is life after death. He did not have to talk to me about it; I simply felt that he knew.

Sitting in the pew for the first time since my son's funeral, I was compelled to look up. There is a window high above the altar, and my eyes became fixed on it. Now and again, I could see a white cotton-like cloud move across the blue, sunlit sky. I still have an uncontrollable urge to look up at that same window each time I enter the church. As I look up I feel anticipation building within me and I know that some day I will see Brian's face smiling back down at me through that window. As I looked up, I felt closer to God, Heaven and my son.

Just before I moved from Prince Albert, a woman I knew stopped by the jewelry kiosk and said, "When you arrive in Kamloops, look up the Compassionate Friends Group. They are a group of bereaved parents who meet to help each other. They are world-wide, and they will help you with the loss of Brian."

I didn't forget what she had said.

About three weeks after we moved to Kamloops, on a day when I felt particularly desperate and very alone, I took out the local telephone directory and looked up the Compassionate Friends Organization. To my surprise, there was a Kamloops chapter. For several hours I debated about phoning, then made up my mind to give them a call. Two things I knew for sure; they couldn't do anything over the phone, and I could hang up if I chose. I carefully dialed the number and listened as the phone rang. I half hoped that the line would be busy, or that no one would answer. As my mind raced, trying to think what I should say if someone did answer, I heard a soft voice on the other end say,

"Hello."

It was Carol, head of the Kamloops Chapter of Compassionate Friends. She was so soft-spoken, and had such an approachable manner, that I liked her immediately and hoped we would become friends. As we talked, the quiet and supportive tone of her voice told me that I had found someone who understood. I made arrangements to go to the next meeting. I didn't know if Ian would be open to the idea of going to a meeting with other parents who had lost children, but I hoped he would. I now realize that I had just completed one of the most important phone calls I had made since Brian died.

That evening, when he came home, I told Ian about my conversation with Carol. I explained how understanding Carol was, and how other men go, too. I explained that everyone who attends the group's meetings has lost a child at some time. I held my breath as I waited for his response.

"If you want to go, we'll give it a try. I'm not so sure about these things, but we can at least go once."

We still attend meetings of the local chapter of Compassionate Friends. Carol has become a close friend and a very important part of my life in Kamloops. Today I am very thankful that I made that first phone call.

January was not an easy month for me. I had no job and I had not had time to make new friends; I was alone each day while Ian was at work. I was miserable. I had no desire to get out of bed. All I could focus on was Brian and that I had lost him. I was a very selfish person during that time, dwelling only on my loss and not considering how fortunate my son was to no longer be sad or ill. I was consumed with grief. I looked forward to the end of each day when my husband would return to spend the evening with me. I began to think, "What if something happens to him too? Then I'll be all alone." I made myself sick with worry.

As often as we could afford it, my friend Christine and I would talk on the phone. I phoned Rebecca and Alain at every opportunity, begging them to move out to British Columbia to be near me.

"You can come back, Mom," said my daughter. "Just move back if you don't like it out there. Your house isn't sold yet. You could move back in and start a daycare again."

"I wish I could, Beck," I answered, "but I can't. I have to stay in Kamloops with Dad. He tried commuting before Brian died and it was too hard on him. And, I can never move again. Brian is buried here and I promised myself I'd never let him out of my sight again. I have to live near him always. I can never move and leave him here; I promised your brother and myself. I don't want ever to let him down again."

Christine had a special feature added to her telephone service. She called first thing each morning to make sure I was awake and out of bed and to find out what my plans were for the day. I soon became very dependent on her.

I continually wondered what great harm I had done in my life which would cause it to be so wretched now. I knew that over the years I had done some wrong things, but most of the time I had tried to be fair. I knew I always gave to people less fortunate than myself, and I loved children and animals. I tried to be an active volunteer in the service of my community and had always been the best mother I knew how to be for my three children. Why had life been so seemingly cruel to me in the past several months?

What would I have done without the phone calls from Christine? Ian let me have the same special long-distance calling feature, while Alain and Rebecca made similar arrangements. Now Becky and I could talk regularly. Michael, too, was phoning often, which was new for him and something I really liked. Frequent personal contact with my two remaining children was essential to assure me that they were safe and well. I still wished that they would both move their families to British Columbia, but I also understood that this could not happen. I knew that whether they lived with me, next door to me, or a thousand miles away, our destinies were already mapped out for us. When it is our time to leave this earth, we must leave. No force can alter this, except perhaps God.

It helped that we started attending Holy Family Church regularly. I still didn't know many parishioners but I did feel very close to God and to my son whenever

I was inside the church. I had begun attending church with my father when I was very young, but I felt closer to God in this church in Kamloops than in any place of worship I had ever attended. I felt I belonged here.

Soon I met Margaret. She always stopped and spoke kindly to me, and before I knew it, she was taking me to meetings of the Catholic Women's League. She invited me to join and, although I had never before belonged to this organization, I agreed. I hoped I could live up to their expectations.

I desperately needed a friend and I was grateful for Margaret's kindness to me. After spending some time in her company, I learned that her daughter had died at the age of two-and-half. I was able to talk to her about Brian, but she seemed so strong and I felt so weak that I wondered sometimes what was the matter with me. Margaret is a wise woman who knows and understands many things. It was she who helped me grasp that Brian was now my guardian angel and that he would always look out for me. Margaret explained that if ever I needed Brian's help I only had to ask and he would be there. She is the one who told me to remember that Brian no longer experienced pain or sadness, only happiness and beauty.

"Kathy," she said, "you are so lucky you will always have a teenaged son to love you. Brian will never grow old. He will always be the way you remember him—a handsome young man with big brown eyes and a beautiful smile. That will never change. So, when you remember Brian, remember that he is your teen-aged guardian angel for eternity." Margaret is so wise. I cherish every moment that I am blessed to share with her. It is thanks to my beautiful son that I came to know such a caring person as my friend Margaret. A short time later I learned that she had sung in the choir at Brian's funeral.

In mid-January, Ian and I went to New York to celebrate my parents' fiftieth wedding anniversary. It was difficult to be cheerful for all those people whom I felt would be watching to see how I was coping. My oldest son was there with his two children—the grandchildren that I had not seen for two years. My daughter and son-in-law were there with their children, and this was the first time we had all met since Ian and I had moved away from Prince Albert.

We were all glad to see each other. My two brothers and seven sisters had brought their children and grandchildren and only one of my nieces was unable to be there. Brian had talked so excitedly about going to New York to visit his relatives, many of whom he had hardly known. He was so looking forward to being included in the photograph showing four generations of our family. He couldn't wait to let everyone see how well he was doing. Everybody seemed to be there except Brian.

I knew how much Brian had wanted to be in that family picture, so I did what I could to make this happen for him. I took with me to New York a twelve-inch by sixteen-inch picture I had showing Brian, myself, and my parents and I stood holding this photo when the anniversary picture was taken. So Brian had his wish and was a part of the fiftieth anniversary family photo, and I know that he was also there in spirit. Then I had one more thing to do.

I had planned that, while the photographer was available, I would have a photo taken showing my three children together. I still wanted to do this. It would be the last photograph of all three of my children which would ever be taken. I asked that Michael and Rebecca be photographed standing about two feet apart. The photographer thought my request unusual, but after I had explained my plan he positioned my two older children and took the picture. When the proofs arrived, I had the last photograph of Brian that I had taken superimposed on the area between the images of his brother and sister. The photo studio did a great job, and hanging in my home, I have that last group photograph that Brian had asked me to get. It is a reminder of three beautiful children and the joy each one has brought over the years.

As January drew to a close, I continued to live in my own personal hell. I pined for something that could not be. Repeatedly I asked myself what I could or should have done differently. I cried all the time when I was alone and also many times when I was in conversation with Christine on the phone. She talked me through it. I went from my bed to a chair. I sat looking out at the sky, hoping for a glimpse of my son—some sign that he was out there and OK. I longed for one of his big hugs, or a "Don't worry, Mom. I know what I'm doing."

I wondered if life would ever return to normal for us. And what was meant by "normal," anyway? Normal, as I remembered it seemed so far in the past.

I just existed day by day. Ian tried both to spend time with me and keep abreast of his work. Our life was a mess. I wanted to keep alive the memory of Brian, both for myself and for all that knew him. I was afraid lest friends and family would forget him. I had never dealt with death before, and I did not know how to begin.

Ian and I went together to our first Compassionate Friends meeting. We were unsure about what to expect, but I was desperate for someone to talk to. That first meeting was hard for both of us, to walk through the door took all our courage. But once there, we felt we belonged for others present understood our hurt and misery and shared our grief. In turn, we each spoke about our lost child. We all shared stories of our children as we remembered them. Everyone was at a different level of recovery from grief, but we could all relate to each other's pain. It was good to be told that there would be a day when we would laugh again, a time when we would be able to remember Brian with joy. Ian and I learned that the sorrow we were enduring was for our loss and ourselves not for Brian. Deep in my heart, I knew that where Brian is, there is no sorrow, there's only joy, happiness and fulfillment.

It was by attending the meetings of Compassionate Friends that I learned more quickly to cope and to understand that I was not alone. I found great comfort in those meeting rooms knowing that I was free to cry, laugh, or remember. Ian and I were given both emotional support, and written information about death and children. The organization had many books available for members to borrow. This was when I came to know that so much had been written on losing a child, on grief and on coping with exceptional stress in our lives. I knew I wanted to read it all, but that would come later. First, I had to get a better understanding of my feelings. I had to focus on what would be the best help for me at this stage in my grieving. I needed to get away. I needed to have a break from this day-after-day loneliness which consumed my every waking moment.

I told Ian I desperately wanted to go back to Prince Albert to be with my friend Christine. I wanted to see Rebecca and my grandchildren. I wanted to hold them, and play with them, and know that they were well. Ian made the arrangements. I flew to Saskatoon, and Christine met me at the airport. I was so glad to be back in the place that I thought was home—back to where I had raised Brian. I believed this would be the answer to all my problems.

Well, I was wrong. I was comforted by the visit to Rebecca and her family and I loved visiting my friends—but something was missing. Life had not stood still while I had been away. Everyone else's lives had kept right on moving while I was stuck in limbo, wanting and wishing for what could never be again. I attended what used to be my regular Al-anon meeting and it was not the same. There were lots of new faces and I felt as though I had been away for a lifetime rather than a mere six weeks. I felt as if I was watching a movie in which some of the characters were unfamiliar to me.

I had a great visit and time passed too quickly. When the week was over Christine drove me back to Saskatoon to catch my plane. I was sad to leave everything for a second time, but the second time was easier.

This time I was glad to be going 'home' to Kamloops. This was where Ian was and where Brian had been buried, and whatever might be in store for me there, Kamloops was where I was meant to be. As yet, I did not know why I was there, but I knew it was where I now belonged and that in time I would come to understand why Brian had been so insistent that I live in Kamloops and why our destiny had brought us to this city in British Columbia.

When I returned to Kamloops, however, I continued to feel sorry for myself. Christine, seeing the mess I was in, started phoning me every morning. She would ask me, "So, what are your plans for today?"

I would usually respond with my now familiar litany of miseries and close with, "Do you see any reason why I should be thankful for yet another lonely day?"

"Yes." replied Christine sternly. "You're alive. You have people who care about you, and you have a husband who depends on you. Oh, and in case you've forgotten, you have children, grandchildren and friends who love you. Now, get up and clean house, or work on your book, or look for a job to occupy your time. Whatever you have to do, do it, but get up and stop feeling sorry for yourself; it won't change a thing. And remember, Kathy, Brian is living in Heaven now. He is happy and he will never know pain again. Brian will never be sad or sick again. Brian will always love you and you him, but just not in the way you were used to. Brian will always be in your heart. Don't you think that if he sees you crying all the time, it will make him sad that you can't accept his happiness? Try to think of him and of your family and get out of bed. Do it for Brian."

I thought a lot about what Christine had said and I knew she was right. It was easier to say than to do, but I tried to pay attention to what she had told me. She was my lifeline to healing. The more I thought about what Christine had said about Brian, the more I knew she was right. Brian had always been sad when he saw me cry. He'd say, "Please don't cry, Mom." I knew it broke his heart to see me in tears, especially when it was over him: not knowing how to help him; kids teasing him; teachers being cruel to him. I had shed many a tear for my precious Brian and had said many prayers that his life would be easier and happier. And now it was—and I was still crying. When would it end?

I wondered what my life would have been like if Brian had died as a result of a drug overdose, or because of an accident resulting from alcohol abuse. Wouldn't the pain have been worse? I recalled the first words I said to Ian when he told me Brian had died.

"Please tell me it wasn't drugs or alcohol. I'd die if he wasted his young life. Oh please, don't let it be that!"

And so, that was my answer. Brian had to change his life before he died so that I could go on living. He had to keep his promise to me to be free of drugs and alcohol. Would he have gone back to substance abuse had he lived? I guess only God and Brian can answer that. I believe Brian knew he would die soon so he did the one thing that he knew I prayed for; he became clean and sober, and he left this world at peace with his life and with himself. He knew he had made me proud of him.

And in death, as in life, that was typical of Brian that he should strive for the happiness of others. Brian had lived ten lives in those short eighteen years, ten lives of suffering, illness, sadness and anger. He had endured much, and he was ready to exchange his life of endurance for the beauty of Heaven. I had to keep reminding myself that Brian had earned Heaven. I was the one not ready for his untimely death, not my son. For Brian was ready, I'm sure. I know he called his friends and family and told them to remember he had made it. I can still hear the pride in his voice as he said, "I made it, Mom. I'm doing what you sent me to school for. I'm a real logger now!"

I passed time by finishing Brian's room. I carefully placed all his belongings in his room in our home in Kamloops just as he had arranged them when he was sixteen and living with us in Prince Albert. I hung his pictures. I framed all his awards and hung them; then I hung his pin collection and all his wrestling medals and Sea Cadet badges. Next, I put in his room a clock that had stopped working. This represented time stopping on this earth for my son. I put a 1998 calendar in the room, and circled October 25, the day of his death. I did these things hoping that some day they would remind one of my children or grandchildren of the beautiful young man, their brother, their uncle—Brian Thomas Roberts, whose life ended too early. I wanted everything to represent what should have been and what would never be. I wanted the whole world to stop as mine had. I didn't want anyone to forget and I prayed I would never forget his face, his smile, his big brown eyes or the wonderful sense of humour, which he saved for me and for his special friends.

I needed everything to be just perfect in case he came to visit his room. I wanted him to feel welcome and at home in our house in Kamloops, to know he would always have a place in my home and my heart. I added all his favorite knick-knacks. There was his "Goofy" collection, his autographed baseball and hockey stick, and "Elly"—the stuffed elephant that he always slept with. I filled his closet with his favorite clothes, including all the club and sport uniforms he had owned since he was born. Then I added all the toys that I had also saved since he was born. Why had I saved all these mementos of Brian's childhood? I certainly had not done this for my two older children, but I had always had a need to hoard everything of Brian's. And Brian, from his earliest years, would say, "Mom, don't give that away! Save it for my kids." So I did.

There would be no child of his to receive these precious things. But I had put them in this, his very own room in Kamloops; and I also had my memories. I prayed I would never be stricken with Alzheimer's disease for if I were who would remember him as I remembered him. Lastly, I made up Brian's bed with linen I felt he would like then set out his favorite stuffed animals, including his adored "Elly" to await his return. At the last moment, I had a telephone connected to the jack in his room. I hoped he would call me some day, and he would need a phone to do that. Countless times I entered his room, picked up the receiver and hoped to hear his voice say, "Hello, Mom. I miss you and love you lots." So far this has not happened, but who is to say it will not happen in our future.

I have spent many hours in Brian's room looking through his photograph albums. I lay my fingers on the image of his face as it smiles his wonderful smile back at me; I see the sad eyes of his troubled years. I love touching his clothes and hugging his stuffed animals. Only the funeral album filled with the cards, letters and poems from his many friends bring me back to the reality of Brian's death. Brian is with God where he will never again be teased, tormented or ridiculed. For in Heaven all are equal and all are kind and loving towards each other. It is the perfect world—the world which Brian longed for all his life, and now it is his for eternity.

As February moves into March, I try to look forward to the beauty of spring. I notice flowers popping through the ground and leaf buds swelling on the trees. This renewal of beauty reminds me that one day I will feel less numb, I will enjoy life and I will find happiness. But still I wonder, "Why Brian? Why now?" When worry about the future of my other children and about my grandchildren creeps into my life, I remind myself that it is not up to me, for it is all in the plan.

New life begins everywhere, but not for me. There are nesting birds, burgeoning plant life and even butterflies emerging from their cocoons. But for me life stands still; I continue to live in a past life in which I had a young son who may have given me a few grey hairs but who was, nonetheless, very special to me. I still look for Brian in every young face I see. I try to trick my mind into believing that Brian is still alive. Maybe he is just hiding, waiting for me to find him as I did in childhood games of hide-and-seek? Soon he would come home and I would scold him for having stayed hidden for so long.

In the midst of these mind games, the phone would ring. It would be Ian, telling me he was on his way home for lunch and I would snap back into the reality of making lunch for my husband and accepting that Brian would never come home again.

And so the months passed. I cried lots. I liked to sit by the window looking out at the sky; perhaps I might have just a glimpse of Brian through the clouds. How I wanted him back!

I still did not know many people in Kamloops. Ian came home at lunchtime to break my day. He was working fewer hours than he had worked in Prince Albert so that he could spend more time with me, but even this did not seem to be helping me much. I was in a place I couldn't get out of.

I finally came to a decision. If I were ever to get out of the rut I had trapped myself in, I would have to finish my first book, *Brian's World*.

Proofreading *Brian's World* was difficult as it brought back so many memories—some of them sad, many of them happy. But both the writing and the remembering were agents of healing for me. The task brought a measure of reality into my life, but it also meant my life was consumed with Brian.

I was still living through Brian and Ian found that very difficult to handle. Gradually, he began to work longer hours.

"I feel like you only wanted to live so you could be with Brian," he said. "He was not the only person in your life. Sometimes I wonder if Brian was the only person in the world you could ever love."

This was not the case, although it seemed that way to Ian. It was only that I had lost the one person who had needed me so desperately, and I had not been able to do anything to save his life. Consequently, I hated myself and questioned the success of my role as a mother and as a person. I wondered how anyone could love someone as much as I loved Brian without realizing how ill he was. It wasn't that I didn't love Michael and Rebecca and Ian, but that I felt unworthy of the love of others. I also thought I would never work again.

I visited Hillside Cemetery regularly. I would stand and look at the bare ground where my son was laid to rest and would wonder as Brian had wondered years ago, "Is it cold when you die? Does it hurt? Is it dark? What is it like in Heaven?" And now I added new, important questions.

"Is it as beautiful as I told you, Brian? Can you see me, Brian? Can you hear me? Do you know I'm thinking of you?"

I knew already that he was safe with God, and there would be only a few more months of asking before I would have the answer to my questions, "Can you see me? Can you hear me?"

In response to Christine's constant, if relentless, encouragement I began the editing of *Brian's World* and so kept my mind busy. I found time passed more quickly while I did something worthwhile during those few moments each day. As I became more engrossed in the task of editing, I realized I had many, many hours of work ahead of me. I set myself the goal of completing my task by Christmas. I made up my mind to have the book edited, in the hands of a publisher and printed before the first anniversary of Brian's death in October. Soon, the few minutes spent each day on the book became a few hours. I had to do this for Brian and for myself. I wanted to remember everything about Brian and his life, and to write it down so that I would never forget. So that no one would ever forget the boy called Brian.

At this stage of my grieving I still worried constantly that I might close my eyes and not be able to see my son any more. I wondered if it would hurt him if I enjoyed life again. I wondered what was expected of me. I wondered how other parents coped with the loss of a child—that most difficult of all losses.

At meetings of the Compassionate Friends group I had heard many parents say that the grief we feel on the death of a child does get less, that we do go on living, and that life does grow easier. But they also said that life is never again the same. I did not expect my life to be the same after Brian's death.

As I began the task of proofreading *Brian's World*, all my precious memories came flowing back. Some were happy, some were sad, but all were worthwhile. Although both the remembering and the writing were hard for me, they were also healing. They were activities I needed to carry through to completion. I continued to live through Brian and, although Ian said little, I could tell by the sad look in his eyes that I made him feel very helpless. It was painful for him to see what was happening to me and to have to stand helplessly by. I think that Ian felt that I, in some way, blamed him for the death of our son. And to some degree, he was right—I did. I needed to blame someone, and who better to blame than Ian. Why could he not have saved my son? Was he not supposed to protect us? Hadn't he seen how ill Brian was during the last few months of his life? Ian, after all, had moved to Kamloops in September 1998 and had spent time with our son. Had he not seen the signs?

The details and sequence of the events of the past six months were now all so jumbled in my mind, and so difficult to set apart from my daily living. Deep down I knew it wasn't Ian's fault, but I needed someone to blame, and I began to wonder if I would ever learn to forgive my husband. I know Ian often felt I only loved Brian, but that was not the case. My son had very much depended on me and I had been unable to keep him alive. I hated myself; I questioned my worth as a mother. But then I remembered what the coroner had told us:

"It is possible that when you thought Brian's behaviour was that of a drug addict, he was instead having a type of seizure which was not drug-related"

Maybe it was a case of not recognizing the symptoms, rather than not being aware of my son's illness.

I still prayed every day for Brian as I did when he was alive, only now instead of praying for his health and recovery, I prayed that he was safe and happy. I wondered if it was too much to ask God that Brian be allowed to come back to say goodbye, to touch my hand, to give me one last hug. I prayed regularly that Brian be allowed to bring me home when it was my turn to go to my eternal reward.

Day in and day out I tortured myself by going to the cemetery where I would stare at the bare ground marked only by the angel stepping-stone. I was anxious for the headstone to be in place. I was sure Brian would understand our great respect for him when he saw the beautiful memorial we painstakingly had designed for him. It would have his picture and that of his friends made into it.

In Brian's Name: Keeping His Memory Alive

In Brian's Name: Keeping his Memory Alive

Ian came home one day and found me in a tizzy; I was trying to accomplish all the Brian-related goals I had set for myself.

"You're obsessed with Brian," stated Ian. "You need to slow down or stop, and take a good look at what's happening in your life. The way you run in circles, trying to do hundreds of things at one time—all for Brian! Brian is gone, Kathy. And no matter what you do or how fast you do it, you will never bring him back again. These work projects are for you, not for Brian. Brian is gone and he won't be coming back."

I have to admit that Ian was right. I was obsessed and did not know how to end this pattern of behaviour. Brian gave me a reason to go on, so I needed to keep him alive.

As April came to a close, Ian brought me a puppy. I think he agreed to the puppy in the hope that it would occupy my time and give me some relief from my obsession. Indeed the puppy did keep me busy, but I compensated by working ever harder at my little projects.

It was at this time that a swimming pool was installed on our property. I begged Ian to have a pool put into our yard because Brian had enjoyed swimming so much. There had been a pool in the yard of our home in Saskatchewan, and many of my fondest memories were of Brian and Ian playing there. I needed to recreate that memory in Kamloops. I hoped that when Brian visited he would feel very much at home, if his surroundings were similar to those in which he was raised. I'm sure now that Brian did not care about where we were; he cared that we were, and that we loved him and missed him.

Besides being busy with these many projects, I still looked for Brian's familiar face in every young person I saw. So, needless to say I was elated when the company installing our pool hired a young man named Jamie who joined the work crew in our back yard. Jamie was about Brian's age and build, and I could tell from observing him that he too had troubles in his life. As the days passed, Jamie and I became quite friendly and I learned that, in fact, Jamie had known my Brian because they had friends in common. Jamie also knew of Brian's death, although when he began working for the pool installation company he had no idea that he was working at the home of Brian's parents. Jamie had come through many troubles for one so young; like Brian he had explored the use of drugs, had experienced living on his own and, also like Brian, he was headstrong and hot-tempered. Jamie was now trying to change his life for the better, just as Brian had been trying to do when he went to the logging camp.

For the next two weeks, the topic of conversation at our dinner table was Jamie. I told Ian what Jamie liked and didn't like; who his girlfriends were; even the difficulties he had with his parents. It was like having Brian back at home for a few hours each day. I rose earlier in the morning so that I could chat with Jamie when he arrived and before he began the day's work. I even kept a supply of sunscreen for his use so that his skin would not get burned while he worked under the hot sun.

One afternoon, the owner of the company installing our pool confronted me. "Jamie is here to work, not to visit. He's also not a child, so you don't need to mother him. He needs to grow up and work like a man."

I was quite upset by these comments, especially as I could see how unfair the company owner was being towards this great kid who only needed to be given a break. And I could also see what a good worker Jamie was. I saw Brian in him; again I experienced all the sadness I had felt every time Brian had been treated unfairly. By the end of the second week of working in our yard, Jamie's boss was relentless in his negative criticisms of Jamie and Jamie's efforts to work well. I repeatedly explained that Jamie was working well and working hard, but on the Friday of his second week with the crew, Jamie was fired.

On the following Monday, I asked why Jamie had not come to work and the other employees told me he had been fired. I was devastated. Jamie's employer just didn't understand Jamie (Brian) as well as I did. I tried to explain that, from what I had seen, Jamie had been his best employee. Jamie had told me during the week that he felt he would be fired on the Friday. I was so angry at the way the owner had treated a troubled youth.

I wept over the loss of Jamie from my life. It was as if I was losing Brian all over again. I wondered why Jamie's boss had not tried harder to understand Jamie. Why couldn't everyone see the good I saw in these boys? I have not seen Jamie since, but I still think of him and pray that he is succeeding.

Why must people be so cruel, I wonder? Why can they not take the time to understand what lies behind trouble and confusion? Why not show compassion instead of subjecting to ridicule? Why not build and restore self-esteem rather than instilling and reinforcing low self-esteem? How can our young people grow to wholeness if no one cares and no one gives them a chance to prove themselves? I wished I could help them all.

After meeting Jamie, my obsession about helping kids like Brian became even stronger. I wanted to save every street kid and I wanted to do it for Brian and in Brian's name. I made plans to open a restaurant for troubled young people. I began to prepare a business plan, researched prices of food, supplies and equipment, examined available real estate, and called every government agency I thought appropriate in my quest for funding for troubled youth. I made very little progress—but I was persistent!

Easter was coming and for the first time in our life together, Ian and I would be alone. Our older children lived too far away to make visiting feasible. Brian had always loved Easter; I could not contemplate the idea of celebrating it without him. I had to do something for Brian for Easter. I drew a very large Easter bunny, which Ian used as a template. I painted the wooden bunny he cut for me, and wrote upon it our Easter wishes to Brian. This we took to the cemetery. This small gesture lifted my spirits a little, although tears still came on the slightest provocation.

Easter was dismal. Deep down I persisted in the belief that, if I prayed long enough and hard enough, God might return Brian to me, if only for a moment. But in the moments when I could face reality, I knew this to be impossible. I had to remind myself often that the signs I received from Brian and the dreams I had about him were God's way of letting me know that my son was well and safe in Heaven. But the signs were not enough. I wanted stronger evidence, and I wanted it more often. I was impatient. Then, when I felt I would never receive another sign, another one was given to me.

But for the moment, I needed more. I had to fill the void left by Brian's death. I needed to feel needed again. The little gestures helped, but the big endeavors took time and money, and I was short of both. It was imperative that I do something tangible, something which I could see and point to and know as a special work which I had completed for Brian.

Because Brian had loved nature all his life, and because he found joy in the beauty of the world we live in, I decided to plant a garden for him. I had hated gardening since my early childhood, yet here I was, digging and planting and caring for what would be a beautiful garden for my son. I knew he would love it and I enjoyed watching nature take its course. Tending Brian's garden brought me the gift of serenity; it also gave me time to think and to slow my pace of obsessional activity. The garden brought me back to nature—brought me closer to Brian.

The exact setting and aspect of Brian's garden was of paramount importance. We have a large yard, but the choice of location would make or break the natural beauty I hoped to enhance. I chose a spot beside our pool. It is a place which overlooks the mountains and the river and thus gives Brian the beauty of the land he loved, as well as breathtaking sunsets and sunrises which dance across the sky.

Soon I was photographing those same sunsets and sunrises. I think of these rolls of film as being imprinted with pictures from Heaven. I know my increased awareness of the beauty of the earth around me is sent to me by Brian to help me see what he saw all along. Peace, tranquility and beauty, a world where everything is wondrous and where all people are equal. And now, first thing each morning, and at sunset every evening I look out at the sky to see what Brian has sent me. I note how beautiful the world is, beautiful like my memories of my son. When he passed away Brian gave me the gift of seeing.

Brian's garden is directly in front of our patio doors. I planned a waterfall that will playfully tumble into our pool. The little falls use water which is taken from the pool and which returns to the pool. Above the waterfall, I planned to put a white Italian marble angel that I purchased shortly after Brian's death. The angel looks like Brian when he was a very young child.

It was all coming together now: the pool, the flower gardens, the waterfall, the trees and shrubs, and the natural beauty of the land—all things that Brian had loved as a child. Maybe my life was coming together again too?

This I do know; every bush, flower and seed I planted in Brian's garden grew tenfold. I remember thinking that I had never before seen marigolds so tall and so stately. Some grew to be over four feet in height. Each week, from March until the date of Brian's birthday in mid-November, I was able to take flowers from Brian's garden to the cemetery. When my grandchildren visit, they wander through this unusual garden. They love to look for the many hidden animals, signs, stepping-stones and wind chimes which help make this a very special place for our whole family. And Brian's marble angel overlooks it all.

The garden kept me busy for most of the summer. But still I was lonely. I seemed unable to overcome the sadness I felt. Smilingly, I would remember the happy days we had spent together. Then my head would fill with thoughts of things, which would never be again, things which, for Brian, would never be.

At last, on a bright sun-filled day in May, the headstone for Brian's grave arrived. Eagerly I waited for it to be laid. Now Brian's resting-place would forever be marked for all to see. The memorial was perfect. There, looking back at me, was one of my favorite pictures of Brian. I felt much more peaceful knowing the headstone was there for him. I'm certain he loved the nature scene, and I'm sure he especially loved the picture of his friends, a reminder to all that he had indeed accomplished the one thing which meant most to him, the joy of true friendship

As Mother's Day drew nearer, I longed for a gift from Brian. I wished one would arrive, even if by mistake. I wished for a phone call, because the sound of his voice would let me know he was with me still. It didn't come and sadness again engulfed me.

And in my renewed misery I once more asked myself all the unanswered and unanswerable questions—all the "if only" statements with which I had indulged my feelings of guilt for the past six and a half months. I was on a downhill slide of self-pity, grief, sorrow and self-blame. But as I wallowed along came my other guardian angel—Christine!

"You did what you could, Kathy," she reminded me. "Remember you are human, too." Ever-practical, Christine went on, "Try to understand that Brian was not kind to his body. You never put a drink to his lips and you never lit one marijuana cigarette for him; nor did you tell him he had to do these things. He chose to do these things against your teachings. He was ill. Substance abuse is a disease; it does terrible things to the body. Even although Brian had stopped those things several weeks before his death, the damage had been done to his already weakened body. You couldn't change that. No one could. And remember, Brian never told you he was having seizures again, so how were you supposed to know? You can only pray for his peace and contentment and trust that he knows how much he was loved by you all."

Those words of encouragement did help me to cope. And I did know that when I closed my eyes, I could see Brian with my mind's eye, and hear him with my mind's ear. I could play a video and watch him laughing and playing. But the video had to be turned off from time to time, and I wanted to see and hear Brian every second of the day. So I put pictures of Brian at all ages all over our home.

"It looks like you're wallpapering our house with his picture," remarked Ian.

I half whispered, half shouted, "It's just that I want always to be free to talk openly about my youngest son; I never want him to be a single photo of someone nobody knows anything about. I couldn't bear it if Brian was just another Uncle Clyde or Aunt Catherine, just a photo on the wall. He lived and he was my son, I need people to remember that and not to be afraid to speak his name."

I succeeded in completing the selection of music that would form the sound track for the video of Brian's life. Next, I had to assemble the photographs and video footage I wanted to use. I kept a copy of the taped music in my car as a constant companion until the second anniversary of Brian's death when I retired it to his room to be played only once each year, on the anniversary of his death. The tape reminds me that, despite loss and grief, I am so very lucky to have known such a great person, even if for so short a time. The music reminds me to live each day to the fullest, to be kind to others and to love all things. And finally it reminds me to be thankful for all that I have and all that I am.

During May and June 1999 I let obsessions take over my life and was almost overwhelmed by them. There was planning the restaurant to be named Brian's Place; writing the book, *Brian's World*; making the video about Brian's life. There was putting the finishing touches to his room, and framing and hanging pictures of Brian, including that last photograph of my three children which had been made as a result of the family reunion in New York State. There was landscaping and planting a garden in Brian's memory, visiting the Safe House and trying to help all his friends; and in my spare time I read all I could about life after death. And constantly I prayed for one more glimpse of my son.

Throughout these two months, my obsessive behaviour made me forget about signs, and about the need to maintain patience in order to be open to them. It was inevitable that I would founder. Then one day in September I opened the front door and there stood Carol, my guardian angel and my friend from Compassionate Friends. She spent several hours with me, giving me reassurance, encouragement, and a sense of direction.

"Kathy, you are trying to do too much and to go in too many directions at one time. You have to stop, take a deep breath and decide what is most important to you. Go one small step at a time; you'll arrive at where you want to be when the time is right for you. Don't push yourself so hard, or you will become exhausted and accomplish nothing. You haven't even let yourself grieve yet. Relax, give yourself time; set priorities and go from there. You've got the rest of your life, and you won't forget Brian. Neither will he be forgotten by those whose lives he touched. You're only one person. Not only that, you're the mother. Stop, take a breath, and go from there. I have no doubt you'll make it—but slow down! Take time for you. Right now, you need to heal you."

I listened to the wisdom of Carol and decided she was right. I had been giving myself no time to relax or think or heal. I made up my mind to prioritize the list of things I most wanted to accomplish, and go forward from there.

I made a schedule. I planned when I would read, when I would relax, and when I would work on projects that celebrated Brian's life. My schedule also allowed time for prayer and meditation and, most importantly, ensured that I would give more heed to my living, loving family whose members I had sadly neglected for many months.

Thank goodness for Carol's timely visit. Her warning reminded me that I hadn't given any thought to anyone in my family except Brian since his death—almost since his birth, if truth be told. But still I wondered, "Does anyone miss Brian as much as I do?"

When I searched my soul honestly, I realized that there probably were others who felt his loss as keenly as I did. I just didn't give them a chance to tell me. Margaret, my friend from church, helped me greatly at this time.

"Kathy," she would say, "remember that this we know—Brian is in a better place now. He'll always be eighteen to you. He will be your special guardian angel, forever looking out for you. And that's the good which has come out of Brian's death."

Just when I thought I might be putting my life into a more healthy perspective, an uninvited memory surfaced. As Kamloops celebrated Victoria Day in May 1999, I remembered details from the summer of 1998. I remembered how Ian and I had met Brian at the bus station when he came from the Youth Custody Centre to spend a week with us in Kamloops. Together, we planned to find him an apartment, a new job, new friends and a fresh start. He had been so excited and had been filled with such hope for a great and good life. Where were our shared dreams now? I can only write that I know Brian's life had a purpose. His role was to help us understand goodness, love and the beauty of the world around us. He wanted to teach us kindness, compassion and unconditional love for humankind.

For nearly nineteen years, my life had revolved around the needs and wants of my extraordinary youngest son and I had lost my own reality as I became one with my son. Now, forcing myself to take Carol's wise advice, I tried to find me, and to find a special place in my life for Brian to rest peacefully. I believed I was ready for that next step on my path towards recovery. I wanted to go on living and I now knew I would never forget my son or what he meant to me. But it was time to move slowly forward. I would once again become an integral part of the life of each member of my family. I had to remember they were still living and that they needed me now probably more than Brian did.

And so it was time to surrender some of my obsessions. To put life in it's true perspective. To take a long look at all I was trying to do and see what was healthy for my family and me. To decide where I wanted my life to go from here. I needed to think about reality and feasibility. I couldn't possibly accomplish all my obsessive objectives and do them well. The first step returned me to Carol's suggestion of prioritizing my life and giving up the unattainable.

The Photo
Album

1984

1981

1981 with his elley

Brian & his best pal Jason 1984

Ian & Brian

Brian & Friends

Gramma and
Grampa Kill,
Taylor (back),
Zachary (the
baby) and
Joshua

Amber

Brian & Rebecca

Father Albert, Brian, Bishop
Blais & Deacon Louie

Arron

Beauty surrounds my life

Working as a model Brian - 10 years

Thank you Brian
for the great gift
you have given me!

Brian June 1987

Brian & Squeeky Sept 1989

The eagle that soars freely above our home is a reminder that Brian is also free. He is free of pain, free of anger and free of substance abuse.

Brian left us a very special gift in his friend, Darren. Darren has brought much joy into my life. He is my son's second chance at life. He is a constant reminder of the good our son brought into the lives he touched with his caring ways.

The peaceful beauty that I am now able to see.

Peace &
Serenity
is ours for
the
asking.

The front door of our
home...painted for the
millenium in Brian's memory.

Ballons I let go on
Brian's birthday

Brian's 21st birthday cake given to the local safe house.

1985
to
1988

Brian
&
Taylor
1993

'Nerd Day'
at school

Christmas 1996

With his older brother Micheal 1986

Christa

Jason & Brian

Darren

Saying Hello & Good-bye one last time.

I am now at peace with my world.

Learning To Live Again

My grandson, Brian's namesake, Zackary Brian is proof that life does go on after the loss of a child.

My grandson, Joshua, sits and enjoys his Uncle Brian's memorial garden, though he never knew his uncle.

Learning to Live Again

June found me still in a "sorry for me" state. I attended meetings of Compassionate Friends regularly for at this point it was the help given me by this group which held my life together. I had told myself that I must appear strong. One of my goals at this time was never to cry again at a Compassionate Friends meeting. I thought that an absence of public outbursts of emotion would let everyone know how well I was doing. I was afraid to lower my guard. I thought I should be the one to handle my sadness and loneliness. I tried convincing myself that in the past I had always been in control of my life. I wanted to be strong and in control, even if only in public and around Ian, who seldom showed emotion. I believed that he thought that I was weak for crying all the time. Repeatedly he told me it was time for me to find a job and to do something constructive with my life, rather than sit around feeling sorry for myself. He meant to help me, but at the time I took his comments as a sign that he didn't care about Brian's death and didn't miss our son. Only in the presence of Christine did I dare to say how I really felt. Christine always understood and I'm sure that Carol, too, saw beneath the facade to the hidden, hurting, angry Kathy whom I hoped no one but I knew.

Writing, and working in Brian's garden helped me. I talked to Ian about the possibility of my seeking professional counseling, but he seemed unwilling to discuss the subject. Christine had mentioned grief counseling to me on more than one occasion, and early in June, I again raised the topic with Ian.

"You don't need counseling; we go to Compassionate Friends. And besides, you're doing fine. You just need to get a job. Once you start work again, you'll be busy and forget all about grief counseling. Everything will work out, you'll see. Sitting at home moping doesn't do anyone any good."

I didn't want Ian to think I was weak, or to get angry with me, so I dropped the subject.

I found myself remembering my grandmothers and their lost children. Most often, I thought about my Grandmother Kill and my Uncle Clyde—perhaps because I had been old enough to remember his death, but not old enough to understand my Grandmother's reaction to it. At first, I wondered why I was not strong like her. I had always thought of myself as being a lot like Grandmother Kill—loving life and children and generally being of a happy disposition. Why could I not get past my grief and loss as she had done so many years ago?

One day, as I sat looking at the sky, I got my answer. Grandmother Kill had not been any stronger than I had; nor had she loved her children less. Merely she had been behaving as society expected her to in the early 1960's. I lived and Brian had died in a different time. No one expected that I lock Brian away in a room filled with him where he would be seemingly forgotten by all who loved him.

It took more than a few months for me to understand that I had to express how I had felt, and how I thought Brian had felt, before his untimely death. I wanted the people who had been important to Brian to know Brian's words, thoughts and fears as he had so often revealed them to me during the course of his short life. I was convinced Brian had lived for a purpose, and I was part of the plan. All I had to figure out was the nature of the plan. I was sure that in time, through prayer, I would come to understand my part in the purpose surrounding my son's living and dying.

As mid-June, and Father's Day approached, I was reminded again of how lonely and helpless I had felt on Mother's Day without a card, a phone call or a visit from Brian. To help the lonely hours pass I started writing. I just let my pencil follow my feelings across the sheets of blank paper. I seemed to be watching someone other than me write. I seemed to have thoughts which were not always my own. It felt as if, through me, Brian were telling Ian how he felt about him as his father, as if he were telling Ian that he had tried to be a good and loving son. The penciled words conveyed how much Brian loved and respected his dad and how much he wanted to earn his dad's love and respect. I was astonished at the outcome of the writing. The poem brought tears to my eyes and when I read it to my daughter to hear her reaction to it, she too began to cry.

This poem truly was a gift from Brian to his dad. I had a copy of the poem matted and then framed with the first and last photographs which had been taken of Ian and Brian together and gave it to Ian on Father's Day from Brian. I hoped it would stir memories for my husband, for I so much wanted to hear him say that he, too, missed Brian.

When Ian opened the gift and read the poem it was all he could do to hold back the tears. He hung the poem above the desk in his office, and although he did not say the words I had hoped to hear, I knew by his expression that he thought them. I knew that he too loved and missed Brian.

As the holiday weekend went by, I found myself writing poems from Brian to everyone in my family and also to his former girlfriend, Christa. I even wrote one to myself. The purpose of the poetry was to tell each person how Brian had felt about them. All these writings were spontaneous, flowing ever so quickly onto the page from my pencil. I believe they were written through Brian's love for us all.

These verses which said all that Brian wished to be said are reproduced on the following pages. I feel that Brian, the boy of few words who had difficulty expressing himself to so many people, was instrumental in composing these poems.

REMEMBER ME
(Written for all Brian's friends)

I became a "street kid" of Kamloops. I was born the youngest of an upper middle-class family. Due to several medical problems and my severe learning disabilities, my mom became my protector. Soon, my low self-esteem, along with my lack of ability to fit into a world that didn't understand, consumed my life. And my troubles began. My mom bailed me out and fought for me every step of the way. At age fifteen, with alcohol already a part of my life, the drug scene found me. I never wanted to be a part of it, but it found me. I became angry and got into more trouble. At age seventeen my mom couldn't bail me out any more. I spent ten months in juvenile hall. It was great there. I didn't have to think for myself, my day was planned for me and I fit in. We were all the same there—most of us with learning disabilities and no real social skills. At eighteen, I was free. I couldn't wait. I was going to start a new life—get a job; make my parents proud of me. Wrong! There was no job for me; life is tough. My low self-esteem returned. Drugs started to take over my life again. I desperately wanted to straighten out my life. A friend told me of a logging job. I got the job and left the drugs and alcohol behind me for a better way of life. I never forgot the "street kids" who were my friends—my family on the street. Shortly after I started my new life, I went to sleep and never woke up. Old medical problems took my life. But I need all of my "friends" to know that, although I died of natural causes, drugs and alcohol contributed to my demise. So, to all my friends, remember me; and please, help each other. Drugs can kill. My life had a purpose—to pave the way for all of you.

To my friends and my family
I miss you all
Love Brian.

Dad

You're so very special to me
We did lots together
Don't you see!

Went across the country
on lots of great trips
You stood by patiently
while I practiced my flips

I wanted to be the kind of son
who would make you proud
No matter how hard I tried
I seemed to be under a cloud

Dad, you gave me warm clothes
your love and our home
You gave me your guidance
your car, a job and a loan

We argued, we fought
you thought I didn't care
But through the good and the bad
I always knew you were there

You taught me to love
have compassion, right from wrong
Many a time I took the wrong path
the way back was long

And through it all
I knew you'd be there
You were strong, and you were fair
no other dad can compare

I fought hard on the way back
to earning your respect
You listened, you watched
you never faltered a sec

You gave me the courage
to fight hard and long
To become a man like you
I had to learn to be strong

Now that I'm gone
try not to be sad
You gave me it all
I'm glad you are my dad

My wish was to make you proud, Dad
and I tried till the end
Please remember I love you
you're my father, my idol, my friend

I love you, DAD.
Brian
(Happy Father's Day—June 20, 1999)

MIKE

You were the greatest big brother
For me there could be no other

Though I moved when I was very young
We were ever apart, for our hearts were as one

You taught me that life could be wild and carefree
How to ride a bike, climb a tree, you accepted me as me

With you as my brother, my friend till the end
I could open my heart and my soul, no need to pretend

You met Kim, had Nikki, your life became exciting and zealous
I saw Nikki as a threat, became possessive and quite jealous

As the years went by, we began to grow up, you and I
You became a great dad, I trudged through school with a sigh

I left school, got into drugs, and then there was Christa
Busy lives, no time to talk, years went by, oh how I missed ya

Our lives continued down different paths, there were many
    changes, I recall
A great logger was I when poor choices of friends, landed me in
    Juvenile Hall

I knew then and there it was up to me, my life I had to change
Counseling, anger management, rehab too, time for my life to
    rearrange

Free at last with a second chance, ready and able to start life anew
Life would be better this time, I knew, for my model, my idol, it
    was you

Leaving was hard for me, my brother, my friend
But please no tears, for remember, in life there is no end

Finally I'm happy and content, for in Heaven I'm free
As years go by, please don't cry, we'll be here together one day, you
    and me

I love you Mike
Brian

Becky

We grew up together, you and I
You held me up so, I could touch the sky

Many times you helped take care of me
Fed me a bottle, bounced me on your knee

You never got angry or complained,
When all the attention, I gained
I was the darling, little angel, do you remember
While you stood by quietly, a glowing ember

Modeling, travel, tap too, we were forever together
Our lives were simple then, carefree, light as a feather

We moved across the country, to start our new life
Adventure I thought, as your heart was struck by a knife

In our new home we settled, our lives weren't so bad
The truth was, we had it all, and we loved our new dad

Our lives were fun, so simple then, but you left for university
I wanted to run, angry I shouted, you're so smart and too pretty

I continued school, teachers were mean and kids were cruel
You came back, a teacher you'd be, no I screamed, you represent
    school

I became quiet and withdrawn, resentful of your success
Everybody's life seemed so busy, while mine was a mess

Seeing the truth, you tried to help, not wanting to squeal
Angry and frustrated, I saw your strength, felt like a heel

As I grew older I demanded my way, became a spoiled brat
Seeing through my tears and my fears, you went to bat
A long hard road was waiting, just ahead of me
I needed your acceptance, don't you see

With each struggle I fought, to reach for the top
You watched, you encouraged, I knew I couldn't stop

Finally I made it; I earned your respect
You were happy, gave encouragement, without neglect

From beginning till end, you were my teacher, my mentor, my
    friend
Never forget the laughter or tears, for in time all hearts do mend

Thank you for taking the time, to teach me to live, love, self-rely
For you were the one who held me up, so I could touch the sky

One day we will meet again
For the love of a family has no end

I love you Rebecca and good-bye
Love Brian

MOM

You were always there, my guiding light
You were the one who stuck by the fight

Through my sickness and my health
Through troubled times and wealth

When life's struggles got hard to handle
You prayed harder, lit another candle

"We can make it son", you'd say
Tomorrow will bring us a brand new day

Even through the drugs and alcohol
You were ever at my side, I recall

I could always count on you being there
When people said, "he's evil", you didn't care

They'd say, "that boy needs to go to jail"
Somehow you always found the bail

You always saw the good side of me
I needed you, why couldn't they see

Our lives our hearts, they were as one
You gave me love, you cared, make my life fun

I've gone to be one of God's angels now
But, wherever you are, I'm with you anyhow

Remember me with a smile on your face
Let no one tell you how to set the pace
I will be with you wherever you go
Protecting you from dangers and foe

Though you will shed many tears
Know that I loved you through the years

For there isn't a more caring mom, anywhere
With the heart of my mom, none can compare

We'll be here together by and by
Thank you for my life, I love you, Good-bye

Love Brian

CHRISTA

To my best friend, my dearest Christa
As the days go by, I really miss ya

You were the one who understood
Never once calling me a geek or a hood

It was too brief, the time we had together
When you were with me, life couldn't have been better

No parents to boss us around
No one screaming "Turn that music down"

We played all night and slept past noon
We hardly saw the sun, but loved the moon

Soon things changed, money was tight
Parents stepped in to help, we began to fight

Our lives became a mess, we lived in a party house
Drinking, drugs and friends took over, what a louse

With no other way out, mom sent me to logging camp
A chance to start anew, my life I had to revamp

We missed each other, for us there could be no other
I called, you followed, with the help of your mother

We struggled, we cried, somehow we couldn't get out
You went back home, I was so angry, I wanted to shout

Somehow we knew we'd never see each other again
Always keeping in contact, I loved you right to the end

Even though I'm gone, my love is still strong
I pray that one day you understand what went wrong

Please remember I loved you and watch over you each day
When you think of me, please smile, no tears, remember what I say

You'll be fine Christa, you'll find your own way
For I'll be your Guardian Angel, forever and a day

I miss you
Love Brian

Writing down these verses really helped me to better understand how Brian felt about those he loved and to this day I feel as if those words were written through me by Brian. It was as if he was beside me, dictating his thoughts, and I was able to capture his thoughts and his way of saying things. I feel that Brian and I are connected. Many times I sense Brian's presence as he gives me ideas, words, or a warm touch.

By late June, I was able to drive around Kamloops—most of the time without becoming lost. I have never been an outstandingly good driver and at that time my mind was further distracted from the task in hand by thoughts of Brian. I would be mesmerized by the beauty of the sky. My concentration was not on my driving and many times my mind would snap back to reality just in time to avoid an accident, to find that I had almost overshot the turn I was supposed to take, or to abruptly come to a halt at a light which had turned red.

Many times, I found myself searching the sky instead of focusing on the road. Once I came out of my daydream to find my car entering the exit ramp from the wrong direction. Before I had time to react, my car made a quick, sharp turn and I found myself once more on the correct side of the highway. I thanked Brian for helping me get back on track; I'm sure he was laughing to himself as he looked down and thought, "Mom, how did you ever get a license in the first place?"

In early summer, I told Rebecca over the phone about my plan to try one more time to get funding for "Brian's Place", the restaurant I dreamt of opening for young people in distress.

"Mom, what do you know about the restaurant business?" Rebecca's voice was stern. "You've done childcare and preschool all your life. Running a restaurant isn't easy. Don't spend a lot of money just to lose it. Dad isn't young any more, and besides, Mom, I don't think you should be getting involved with the street kids—you are too soft! You remember how Brian controlled your life, and they will do the same. You will get involved in their lives and the next thing you know, they will be moving in with you, with yet another sad story to tell. Dad will just be upset again, and you two will be arguing again. Please think about it before you do anything you might regret, Mom. Even if you were to open a restaurant, it wouldn't help Brian, and it wouldn't bring him back either. Please take some time and think about it. Maybe you could sell your "Weekenders"? You've had the business for some time."

"I'll think about it, but I can't promise anything. I need people to remember your brother," I continued, "and I don't want his death to have been for nothing. I want his death to help other children like him to have a chance for a better future."

The conversation ended with Rebecca reminding me to take my time and not to jump into anything I might regret later.

Ian was now hounding me to get a job, or sell "Weekenders", or do something. Bills were piling up. There was only one pay cheque coming in and the move to Kamloops had been very expensive for us. In addition to our customary expenses, we had Brian's funeral to pay for, and all his unpaid bills which we had co-signed for him. I knew I had to start working soon.

I did a lot of praying in my search for a solution as to how I could best contribute to paying our family living expenses. As June came to an end, I finally decided to at least check out the cost of having business cards printed so that I could run my "Weekenders" business. On my way to the printing shop, I asked Brian repeatedly what he wanted me to do.

"If you want me to open a restaurant for the kids let me know by having funding become available for it. But if you think I should sell 'Weekenders', please—give me a sign."

All the way to the office of the printing company I continued to ask for a sign. On my way home I was still asking Brian for a sign which would let me know what he felt I should do. Without my planning it, my car turned onto Summit Avenue, the street leading both to the Cemetery and to Ian's office. I thought, "Oh well, it seems my car wants to go this way today. As long as I'm in this part of town, I may as well stop and tell Ian that I've started looking into business card costs."

My thinking was wrong—again! Seemingly of its own free will, my car turned into Hillside Cemetery. This time I told myself, "As long as my car is determined to go to the cemetery, I may as well dump out the stale water from the urn at Brian's grave so that I can bring fresh flowers on Sunday."

As I suspected, the cemetery lawns had been mowed recently and the flowers were gone. I got out of the car and emptied the water from the urn, which I then replaced by the grave. As I did so, and much to my surprise, I heard a tinkling sound from inside the urn. Grumbling to myself about the darned lawn mowers throwing stones onto the graves, I upended the urn on the grass. For a second time I placed the emptied urn by the grave—and for the second time I heard the tinkling sound!

Peering inside, I saw lying on the bottom what appeared to be a ring. I thought it strange that the ring had not fallen onto the grass when I had turned the urn upside down. It crossed my mind that Brian's friends must have left him a ring from a gum machine. They often came to visit and left him items such as cigarettes, lighters, French fries or hair butterflies as tokens of there love for him. I reached down to the bottom of the urn to retrieve the ring and, when I opened my hand, I gasped in disbelief. I shook my head in case I was imagining what I saw, but there it was in my hand—a fourteen carat white-gold ring set with an aquamarine and two diamonds. I closed my hand, opened it, and looked again. It was real.

I whispered, "Thank you, Brian. It's the sign I've been waiting for. I will sell my 'Weekenders'. I just needed your approval on this one."

I tried the ring on my finger. It fitted perfectly.

I returned to the car and went directly to my husband's office, a two-minute drive away.

"Ian! Look what Brian gave me!"

Ian looked at me strangely as he examined what lay in my hand.

"Kathy, where did you get that ring? It's a real ring with real diamonds, you know."

"I know. Brian gave it to me, and it's just my size."

Then I took a breath and told Ian the whole story: about asking for a sign; pricing the business cards; and my car turning into Hillside Cemetery.

When I had finished speaking, Ian looked at me in puzzlement and asked, "You don't think one of his friends stole it and then hid it there, do you?"

I assured Ian that if someone had stolen it they certainly wouldn't have hidden it in a flower urn at the cemetery to be dumped out along with stale water and never seen again.

When both of us had come to our senses Ian said," You're right, Kathy. It is a sign from Brian. He gave you that ring. How else could it have come there? And why else was it exactly your size?"

At home, later in the evening, we had time to talk about the mysterious ring and we worked out its significance. Earlier in the year, I had asked Ian to give me a ring for my birthday, which fell in August. Ian had said that he would have loved to, but that he could not do so this year as we could not afford it. Brian knew that clothes and jewelry were something that I knew and loved as he did. Brian also knew I would recognize the significance of a ring set with diamonds, for when he was a boy he won a necklace of imitation diamonds for me and when he gave it to me he said, "Someday I'll buy you a real diamond, Mom."

Next I called Rebecca and told her the story of the ring. She, too, was very excited for me.

"Mom, I believe in those things, like signs. Don't you?"

I assured her I did; now more so than ever, for now I had proof—proof that my son was well. He was just in a different, non-earthly form. His spirit lives on and he is with me. He had proved to me that there is life after death.

"I'll come at the end of July," continued Rebecca, "and help you get your 'Weekenders' business going."

I thanked her, and then thanked Brian for the best gift ever—the gift of understanding. I put on the ring and have not taken it off since.

Not long after receiving the ring from Brian, Ian and I watched James Van Praagh on television. He spoke about his experiences of communication with the spirit world and told about his book, *Talking to Heaven*. Ian and I bought the book and both of us eagerly read every word. I believe reading this book marked the turning point for my husband. When he had finished *Talking to Heaven*, he said.

"Kathy, you really did get the ring from Brian, didn't you?"

"Yes I did, Ian. I told you he guided my car to the cemetery, and that is where he gave me the ring. He is my guardian angel. He will always be with us, Ian, only just in a different way. But he is still our son—forever."

Silently, we both acknowledged that our son had been communicating with us since his death. All the signs we had received from Brian now had so much more meaning for each of us.

I now understood the source of the words which were the poems that came to me as messages to our family and to Brian's friends. Brian was communicating to all he loved by writing through me. I had never been one to write poetry, or even to be interested in it. Yet, here I was writing verse after verse for those oh-so-important people in Brian's life. Brian had no time to say his good-byes or thank-yous but he was now able to say these and more through me. For in death as in life, Brian and I were still connected; we were as one person.

The Coroner's Report:
Will My Questions Be Answered?

(A similar photo of Jesus was found in my son's belongings after his death...and we have a photo of Brian as a child which resembles the child in this print.)

My son had many questions about death and life after death as he grew up. Now it is my turn to ask those same questions.

The print "In His Light" by Greg Olsen reminds me of how connected my son was to a power greater than ourselves.

The Coroner's Report: Will My Questions Be Answered?

In July, I was still searching for answers. Why had Brian died when he was doing so well? Why wasn't he given just a little more time to enjoy the life he tried so hard to achieve? Didn't my son deserve that chance for a peaceful, happy existence after all the turmoil in his life? But only God has the answers to these questions. I must wait until I meet Him to ask him why my youngest child was destined to die.

My grandson, Taylor, came to spend the second half of July with me, and this helped to pass time. We did many things together for I always enjoy his company. Taylor is such a sweet child and so all-knowing about the world. He also is so very much like his Uncle Brian—a resemblance that is sometimes hard for me to bear. Little Taylor also has learning disabilities and is deficient in some social skills. Each day I can see his uncle in him. Taylor is also the only grandchild I have who knew Brian well. He loved his uncle and spent lots of time with him. We talked a lot about Brian over the two weeks we were together.

I showed Brian's garden to Taylor and told him that whenever he saw a butterfly there he should say, "Hello". I explained that butterflies are a sign of new life and that the butterflies in Brian's garden were Uncle Brian and his friends just stopping to say hello as they admired the beauty of this special garden.

Rebecca came as promised to help me start my "Weekenders" business. Brian had been right to give me the ring as a sign to make this business choice for I never did get any funding for "Brian's Place." I threw out the business plans and all the contact numbers I had gathered in preparing to open "Brian's Place", and gave my complete attention to "Weekenders." Brian gave me the permission, the strength and the courage to begin living and working again. Daily I thank God for the gift of my son.

One summer afternoon while Rebecca was staying with us a small, inconspicuous white butterfly came fluttering through the garden as Taylor and his mother were admiring the brilliantly-colored July flowers.

"Mom, look! Here comes Uncle Brian to play in his garden!" exclaimed Taylor. "He's a butterfly, you know. Grandma told me that butterflies are a sign of new life. She said that whenever I see a butterfly playing in Uncle Brian's garden I should say hello because it's Uncle Brian and his friends coming to play."

Rebecca was impressed by what Taylor remembered, and it warmed my heart to hear my little grandson remembering his uncle in such a special way.

I took to watching in the garden on a daily basis throughout the remainder of the summer. It gave me such pleasure to see the butterflies fluttering and playing as they fed among the flowers and shrubs. Their presence brought Brian closer to me. As fall set upon us, the days got colder and I was saddened by the disappearance of the butterflies. But I knew that with the spring they would again return to play.

All summer I continued to read as much as I could on death, the spirit, and life after death. The signs Brian had sent me had given me hope and a different way of looking at death and life. The sign I most longed for was for Brian to appear to me and tell me he was OK, and that he was alive in spirit and with me always. At church I watched through my favorite window above the altar, always hoping for a glimpse of Brian. What I came to realize, however, was how much was given to me. I began to notice the beauty of the world.

Once I had grasped this real gift of beauty, I realized that Brian was with me in the church. I could feel the warmth of his touch. I could feel his long, thin fingers as he took my hand. And now I understood that I needed not miracles, but reassurance. Each time I entered church I felt Brian take my hand. Then I recalled what I had told Brian when he was in his teens.

"The best gift you can give me, Brian, is to come to church with me."

Brian had always tried to accompany me to church on special holidays such as Easter, Mother's Day and Christmas, and now in death he continued to give me that precious gift of his companionship each Sunday.

Despite the progress I was making in daily living, my life was far from happy. My obsession with all matters relating to my dead son continued. On the most wretched days, I would go up to Brian's room and stare at the picture of him in his coffin. Doing this usually helped me cope with what was real in my life. And my son's death was real.

In late July, the coroner's office telephoned to explain the final results of the autopsy on Brian. It had taken nearly nine months to complete necessary tests and investigations. I had thought all along that, once the coroner's report was filed I would find a measure of peace, but I was wrong in this expectation, for no one really knew for sure why Brian had died.

From the perspective of the medical examiner Brian was a healthy eighteen-year-old male with no noticeable medical problems, and certainly none that would have caused his death. There were no significant amounts of alcohol or drugs in his system, beyond the remains of a marijuana cigarette which he must have smoked the evening of his death. After much investigation, the coroner concluded that Brian may have been experiencing seizures for a while before his death occurred, and that these seizures were not unlike the ones he had as an infant. There was evidence of some examples of unusual behaviour on Brian's part on the evening of his death and the coroner believed that this atypical behaviour may have marked several small seizures. It was postulated that during the night Brian had a more serious seizure which caused his heart to stop.

Now we knew, but did our knowledge change anything? Would knowing the cause of death hasten the process of my healing? The answer to these questions was decidedly "No!" The coroner's findings did nothing to lessen the ache in my heart, and in fact brought more questions for me try to answer. Why had Brian not told me he was having seizures again? Why had he not asked for help, either from a doctor or from myself? Had my son's life been such a torment that he wanted to leave this earth? The coroner's verdict changed nothing.

Now more than ever I was left with unanswered questions which only Brian could resolve. I promised myself I would ask Brian when next I saw him. And when I met God, I would ask Him why he had given me such a wonderful gift as Brian only to take him away at what had promised to be the real beginning of his life. I did know from my reading, however, that there was a lesson to be learned from the life and death of this child.

The release of the coroner's report was followed closely by my decision to make Brian another memorial to be placed in the cemetery during the summer months. I based the memorial theme on a prayer service given by Holy Family First Communicants and I incorporated into the memorial the words from the verses of the song sung by the children.

During the slow months of summer and fall one thought crossed my mind time and again, I did not have to stay here. I could abandon earthly living and join Brian at any time I chose. But would we be together? I knew and believed that it is a sin to take one's own life. If I committed suicide, I would not be accepted into Heaven and I might not see Brian again. I also knew I had a duty of love to Michael and Rebecca which I could not abandon.

So I sat, and rocked, and cried, and remembered that Brian had already given me enough joy and love to last a lifetime. No one could erase the yesterdays with Brian and I would have many tomorrows to share with my living children, my grandchildren, and most of all with my husband. I knew that they should now become the joyful and loving center of my life, but still I found it difficult to focus on how fortunate I was to have so many loved ones who truly cared about me. There were but few times in the year following Brian's death when I was able to express how deeply I cared for my loving family.

Then, while I was working on the manuscript of this book, one of my favorite songs was played on the local radio station. Hearing the lyrics of "*Thank God for Kids*" by Mac Davis helped to put into perspective everyone and everything in my life. The closing verse reminded me that the Lord gives, and the Lord takes away. It's all in the plan.

For our lives are mapped out before we are born, and at times, children will subtly reveal some of what they knew and understood from before their birth. They seem to know without realizing they know. Brian's childhood questions about Heaven and death and the telephone conversation with me on the day before he died are to me indicators of his pre-birth memories. In his own unconscious way, Brain as child and then as young adult was trying to prepare me for what would be his destiny.

In August I had my fiftieth birthday and found myself at a place in my life very different from that which I had planned. Instead of a joyous occasion shared with friends and family and filled with laughter, I had sadness, reflection, and quiet conversation about Brian's death and how hard life had been for my youngest son.

I slipped back into denial—Brian would come back. Many an afternoon I stole quietly into his room and lifted the telephone receiver, just in case he was speaking at the other end. I spent hours alone sitting, rocking, and endlessly listening to the audiotape I had made to accompany the video of Brian's life. Sometimes I would smell a whiff of vanilla pass inexplicably through the room. I love the smell of vanilla and on many evenings, I would light a vanilla-scented candle. But on those afternoons when I played the audiotape, no candle was burning. I always interpreted this phenomenon as a sign that Brian was nearby.

Early in September 1999, Ian took me to Vancouver to watch the Molson Indy car race. I thought about Brian and how much he would have loved to have seen this. The pace car was a Viper—Brian's favorite car. He had told me he wanted to own a Viper some day. So, I asked the driver if he had a photograph of the pace car.

"No," he said, "but I have something better. I have Viper trading cards; would you like a set?"

"Yes, I want them for my youngest son. He loves Vipers."

The driver gave me two sets, saying as he did so, "I hope your son likes the cards. How old is he?"

I looked at him as I thanked him. "He would have been nineteen, but he died a year ago."

"I'm so sorry," the man said quietly.

I think from the look on his face that he didn't know whether to hug me or have me committed! But I was grateful for the cards, and I put them in Brian's room when we got home.

It was now mid-September and I was still struggling. I seemed to be taking three steps toward recovery and six steps back. I just could not accept that Brian was dead. Where to go from here I did not know. I couldn't or wouldn't wake up.

Desperation: Are psychics the answer?

I spent hours looking out at the 'still' beauty of the world around me as I pray for answers. Why when my son's tragic life was finally turning around, why did he have to die?

Desperation:
Are Psychics the Answer?

Late September 1999 found me still searching desperately for an answer to my most urgent question: why had death come like a thief in the night to steal my son? It would soon be the first anniversary of Brian's death and I had been told that if I could it make through the first year after such a loss as I had suffered, the pain would miraculously diminish, and life would reassert itself.

I had been mislead. It was now forty-six weeks since my son had died so unexpectedly and I still grieved as deeply and as painfully as I had on the day I first learned of his death. I needed answers and I needed peace, and I needed these quickly if I was to be ready for the start of year two without Brian.

Lately, the words I had heard spoken during the Oprah Show when James Van Praagh made his guest appearance had been eating away at my soul. Van Praagh had talked about people who had "left the earth plane". He talked about life after death, and he talked about speaking to the spirit world. I kept getting the urgent feeling that I needed to speak to this man, or at least to someone who could reach the spirit world as he could. I needed a spiritual medium—someone with extraordinary psychic ability to act as a channeler.

I tried to reach Mr. Van Praagh, but this was not possible. My only hope seemed to lie in going on one of his cruises. I learned that the upcoming cruises during which Mr. Van Praagh would be giving presentations left from U.S. ports. Passage for a single person cost more than $2000 and no private meetings would be scheduled with Mr. Van Praagh. There was, however, the opportunity to participate in one of his group sessions during which he might or might not be able to reach my Brian. I needed an alternative solution which promised more and cost less. I was desperate to reach my son, if only for a few moments.

I found a telephone number listed in a local alternative health services brochure which came in the mail. I phoned the number listed for Joan, a Spiritual Healer, and left my phone number on her answering machine. Joan phoned back several times over the next week and left messages for me, but I did not return her calls as I had become quite nervous and was now telling myself that I had made a big mistake in phoning her in the first place.

On Thursday September 23, 1999 as I was getting ready to leave on a trip to Edmonton with Ian, the phone rang. I lifted the receiver quickly and was shocked as the voice at the other end of the line said, "Hello. I'm Joan returning your call."

"I'm very sorry, Joan, but I phoned you by mistake. I dialed the wrong number; I'm really sorry to have inconvenienced you."

Quickly Joan blurted, "Wait! I sense you just lost someone very young and very close to you."

Quietly I answered, "Yes. I just lost my youngest son a little less than a year ago."

"I have a message from him for you," continued Joan. "I feel his presence here with us right now."

Joan immediately had my attention and I was more than eager to listen to what she had to say. Joan started by giving me facts about my son and our family, and then went on to give me information, as it was given to her from Brian.

"Brian says to tell you his death was an accident. He says it was time. He wants you to know that he had allergies; he had them for a very long time. You didn't know and neither did the doctors. He didn't feel well for a very long time, but now he's healed and he feels great. Brian says he is with you all the time. He says you'll be fine, just follow your dreams. He wants you to pay attention to life and pay attention to yourself, and that everything will be OK."

There was more. "He says he loves his room. He says he's glad you like the ring. Brian says that if you meditate with the ring, he'll be able to reach you. He says to watch when you burn candles. He wants you to know that he dances in the flame.

"Brian wants you to know that he is in a beautiful place, more beautiful than anywhere you could ever imagine or have ever seen before. He says there are lots of beautiful gardens and lots of flowers, and there are fairies all around him.

"He wants you to know that he always loved you lots and that he is always with you. Brian says that Ian was his dad in a previous life; that's why they are so much alike.

"He says it's not anyone's fault that he died. 'It's not Dad's fault. Dad was trying to protect himself from the pain, and trying to protect you, too. You couldn't have saved me, Mom, the pain would have been too much for me.'

"Brian said he was full of poison due to his allergies. He poisoned his own body until it couldn't take any more. He says it was an accident—an allergic reaction. He didn't mean for it to happen. He says the marijuana cigarette he had that night had something bad in it and he had an allergic reaction.

"He says he's watching over Christa. He wants her to draw an automatic drawing with color. He says all she has to do is to concentrate on him, and he will do the drawing through her. The drawing will show you where he is. He says it's a beautiful place.

"Brian says not to open a business in his name; it will be too painful for you.

"He says for you not to worry; you don't have any cancer. Brian says to tell his dad to stop all dairy products ASAP.

"Brian says that you are just like him; you are both alike. He needs you to know that; and he says you shouldn't trust doctors, but you should get some help.

"Brian wants you to know that a new baby will be conceived in your family. He says the child will be him, and it will give you all that you need. Brian says you will see him through the baby's eyes and spirit. He wants you to know he will be with you always through the new baby.

"He says he wants you to know that he learned his kindness and generosity from you. He says he loved you unconditionally. He says he knows how much you loved him. He continues, 'Mom, you'll have a special bond with that baby. You'll know it's my spirit with you for always."

"Brian says he would rather have been cremated, but you never had a chance to discuss it. But he wants you to know he is happy with your choices.

"He says he is sitting in a beautiful place, a garden. It's beautiful, with lots of green. And he says he's healthy now.

"He asks you to put fairies in his garden.

"He says, 'Don't be afraid to cry, Mom. You have to cry to heal.' He says you're doing fine and that all your medical problems will pass if you let go.

"Brian says, 'Don't blame Dad. Things will get better again.'

"He says he will stop coming to visit after the baby is born, but you will find what you need in this new baby.

"He says, 'I know I was very young when I died, Mom, but I came to you as a special gift. I had something very important that you needed to learn. "

"Brian says his death was very peaceful. He wants you to know he is very happy now. He needs you to know he understands you and loves you so much; he always has. He always knew how much you loved him, too."

I was overwhelmed with all the information that Joan had just given me. We had spent the better part of an hour talking on the phone as she relayed information from Brian to me. I had never in my life spoken to her before that day and I knew the information she was giving me had to have come from my son because there was no other way she could have known many of the things she told me. As we were saying goodbye, Joan said, "There is another medium in town. Her name is Nadine. She is good and probably a little more advanced than I am. She may be able to give you more information from Brian than I could."

Later that same day, as we drove to Edmonton, I fell half-asleep. Ian put a CD into the player and as soon as the music started to play, I woke up. The CD Ian had chosen to play was the sound track from "*City of Angels*", a disc I had purchased a month before so that I could use one of the tracks to accompany the video about Brian's life.

"Did you buy this CD?" asked Ian.

"Yes, a while ago; for the video."

"How did it get in the car? Did you bring it with you?"

Surprised, I answered, "No, you must have picked it up from my stereo in the house."

A puzzled expression came over Ian's face. "But I haven't changed the CDs in the car since our trip to Edmonton back in July."

I thought for a moment. "And I didn't even own this CD in July."

The song named "*Angel*" began to play. This track was the reason I had bought the CD, and at that moment, both Ian and I understood what had taken place. "Brian wanted us to know he was with us, and he knew that causing this CD to be played was a way of letting us know he was here."

It was all coming together now. My life, my son's life, meeting Ian, it all made sense now. Many of the things Brian told me through Joan have happened. On June 10, 2000—almost nine months to the day after my landmark telephone conversation with Joan, Rebecca and Alain had a son who was named Zachary Brian.

The conversation with Joan also helped Ian and me to understand why Brian seemed to know Ian the first day he met him. At the time of their first meeting Brian was six-and-a-half years old; it was August 1986 and we had stopped the car to buy ice cream. As we got out of the car, Brian slipped his small hand into Ian's large one and asked, "Can I have a big cone, Dad?"

I remember that both Ian and I were taken by surprise. It was as if Brian and Ian had known each other all Brian's life. Ian just looked at me and said, "I'm going to be his dad, so I'm glad he accepts me." Now we understood why Brian the small child had spoken as he did; he had known Ian in another life and he also knew that in this life Ian was going to be his dad. Many times as Brian was growing up Ian would say, "I don't know why, but I feel like he is my real son.

We're so much alike. Sometimes I feel like I've known him all my life. I feel we've met before."

I was overwhelmed by everything Joan told me, but I was leery, too. Could Brian really reach me? Before speaking with Joan, I had hoped what I was feeling and seeing was real. Now Ian and I both believed there was a life after death and that our son was now in a better place. We also felt in some ways that he was still with us and could give us messages, if only we took the time to listen and understand. But even the messages from Brian through Joan weren't enough. Now I wanted more. Much more.

For the next two weeks all I could talk about or think about was what Joan had told me about the other psychic in town, whom she believed to be even more advance than she was. I was more anxious than ever for more news from Brian. Carol and Margaret both warned me to be cautious, but I needed to know Brian was OK. All I thought about or dreamed about was seeing Brian again, hearing his voice just one last time. I told Rebecca about Joan and she told me she too believed in spiritual mediums.

It was because of the encouragement and understanding I felt I got from my daughter that I phoned Nadine as soon as I got home from Edmonton. I booked an appointment for the following Saturday. I paced all week, anxious to hear what she would have to tell me. The following is a description of what happened during my visit to Nadine's.

First Nadine said a prayer. Next she told me that her emotions may go from happy to sad, or even to tears depending upon what feelings she would receive from Brian.

Nadine started crying. I almost ran out of the room right then because the whole scene seemed too eerie for me. Then she said, "I get a sense that Brian had a rather sad life. It seems to be filled with turmoil and sadness." As she continued she talked as if she was Brian or whichever spirit she was representing. Mostly she spoke in the first person, for she was usually the voice of whomever she was revealing messages from. She told me to ask questions whenever I wanted to.

Brian:	Mom thanks for coming. I know this is hard for you, but it is a way we can communicate
Nadine:	Brian is standing in a tall forest of some kind. He is showing me that he is in a forest. There is a log in front of him and light—very bright light—just behind the trees. I can see the light through the trees. Brian is wearing jeans, work boots and a plaid shirt. Does this mean

anything to you? I feel a sense of peace through the trees, and I see the sun deep in the forest.

Brian: My guide was here to meet me when I arrived.

Nadine: Would you like me to describe his guide?

Kathy: Yes.

Nadine: His guide is beside him. He is wearing full buckskin; brown buckskin. He appears to be a Native American.

Brian: I'm grateful to my guide for meeting me, he helped me adjust. It's like having your best friend with you all the time. He has taught me lots. When I was first here, I was in shock; I thought it was a dream and I tried to wake up. I saw my body, like you read about in books. My guide helped me.

Kathy: How did you die? Why?

Brian: I thought I had a stomachache. My legs were heavy and my chest was heavy too, like I had food poisoning, or something. I lay down, and I think I fell asleep. The next thing I knew, I was looking down at my body. I tried to wake up but I couldn't. I went up towards a beautiful light. I was in a tunnel and I felt so light; I kept looking back at my body, but I felt so light. I thought I was dreaming.

Kathy: Did he have a seizure?

Nadine: I can see lots of energy in his head. He's showing me lots of energy; it looks like a lightning storm in his head.

Brian: I didn't want you to worry about my seizures. It was embarrassing to have seizures. I didn't want you to worry or make a big deal about it. The seizures made me feel like I was strange or different. Thank you for being a good mom—the kind you were; and for doing your best.

Kathy:	Does he remember the nickname Mike used to call him? And does he remember what he slept with, and what he called it?
Nadine:	Brian doesn't remember the nickname. He is showing me what he slept with. It is hard to see. Is it a stuffed animal of some sort? Is it brown?
Kathy:	Yes, it was a stuffed animal, but it was blue.
Nadine:	Yes! Brian says a blue elephant. He says he called it—it's hard to make out what he's saying—but it sounds like "Elffy".
Kathy:	He called it "Elly", but he had some trouble with his speech. Now that I think about it, his "Elly" was sort of brown. He dragged it around so much, and I had covered it so often, that it was kind of a dirty brown. Mike used to call him "French Fry"; he hated that nickname when he got older.
Brian:	Oh Mom!
Nadine:	(laughing) He's laughing. I'm seeing him with spiked hair. He very definitely showed me himself at a younger age with his hair sticking up on his head. He might have been five or so.
Kathy:	Brian did have his hair spiked when he was seven and he did lots of modeling.
Nadine:	How at peace he is there. He says he wasn't at peace on earth.
Kathy:	Will I see him again?
Nadine:	His soul and heart were very troubled on earth, but he is at peace now.
	He will come to you in your dreams. He says to ask before you fall asleep. You can go beautiful places together. He says he's learning a lot about the choices he made on earth. He said he understands why he was on earth for so short a time. It's hard to explain. He is asking for help from his guide.

Guide:	Thank you for being Brian's mother. We choose our life together before we come to earth; you are celebrated as a mother in Heaven for choosing a child with Brian's problems.
Brian:	I was getting my life together, but I had to leave.
Guide:	We all know our life's plan. Brian knew he was going to die before he died, but he doesn't know if you understand what I mean; it's hard to explain.
Brian:	I love you lots, Mom. Our love is still there; we're still connected. When you think of me, it's because I'm thinking of you. We're more connected now than we were when I was on earth. You give off so much energy.
Nadine:	Your energy color is blue—a beautiful royal blue. It fills the whole house. It's more than your aura; it's a powerful energy. Would you like to know about your guide? She is here.
Kathy:	Yes.
Nadine:	She is very beautiful. Her dress is very long and flowing. Very beautiful. Her dress is exquisite; it's in all colors. She's exceptionally tall; she surrounds you with energy.
Kathy's Guide:	There are so many people with you. You give off so much energy and love. You give so much away. Put some energy into yourself, don't give so much away. You give so much to others. Don't worry about what others think or need; refill yourself. Tears are very healing. Don't be ashamed to cry, they will wash away your grief. Brian and I are worried about you. You're giving too much energy away; you're not keeping any for yourself.
Brian:	Mom, don't judge yourself as to how much time you need to heal. I'm worried about you, Mom. You're giving too much energy to others. You're not saving enough for yourself. You did the best you could do. The reason dad didn't want me at home was because you couldn't help me. It's time to look after yourself.

Please know you are not responsible for my passing. It's just how it was—how it had to be.

Nadine: Do you know a little girl with blonde hair? Brian is showing me her. She is holding a doll.

Kathy: No.

Nadine: Brian is in the forest to heal. He is sitting on a log now with his guide. He is showing me the eagles in the sky. There are eagles flying above Brian; he wants me to tell you they are there.

Kathy: What does Brian think of the book I'm writing?

Brian: I love the book. It is important for other parents. It's good for you to get everything out of your head—to get it on paper. The book is important for Dad, and for Michael and Becky, but mostly for other parents. It will open their eyes and their hearts; it will help them to understand. That is the reason I had to die, so you could write the book. You will be able to speak to many different people because of the book.

Nadine: Brian's telling me that your souls were connected many times in past lives. One time you were Siamese twins. This time, he says, you chose to be here at the same time, but to each be your own individual on earth. He said sometimes this plan didn't work out as expected because you were both such intertwined, connected souls. He is saying that one time you were his guide while he was on earth. You are very close. He says he left earth early to allow you to disentangle yourself from his life. He wanted to allow you to go on alone and live life to the fullest. He realized that you didn't have a life of your own. He was trying to make a life for himself, but you had no life independent of him.

Brian: My death was a gift to you, Mom. I wanted you to discover who you are without me. I took up so much of your space. I wanted to give you the gift of life. It's just a small gift compared to all the gifts you've given me, but I need you to know I wanted to give you this special gift. I want you to discover who you are without me. Dad was my son in a previous life. We were very wealthy and I had very set ideas on how my son's life would turn out. He—my dad, my son—rebelled. He had no interest in my plans for his education. He was a painter and he left and went to France to paint. He cut off ties with the family, so I cut him out of my life. He was very bitter. I understand Dad, and that he feels protective of you.

Kathy:

Please watch over your brother and sister for me. And Taylor—please protect him. He has worse learning disabilities than you did; please look out for him, too.

Brian:

Michael has some things to learn before he gets his life back. Mike must learn to trust that he has changed; he needs to trust in himself. He needs to realize that he is the person he wants to be. Becky was very frustrated with me. She needs you, Mom. Try not to talk about me all the time around her. She feels she didn't get enough attention from you because of me. Don't push her, Mom. Give her time. She is overwhelmed with emotions and angry that I am gone. She also feels some guilt over her jealousy of me. She'll be OK; just give her space without me in it. I'll look out for Taylor, don't worry. He needs lots of help, but the book will help him too. It will help people to understand through the eyes of someone who had learning disabilities. You saw through my eyes, Mom. You picked a good title for the book, *"Brian's World: Can't You See What I See?"* for you truly could see what I could see, couldn't you, Mom? I can't come back for a while, Mom. All the love you send, and the prayers, and all the things you do for me—they are like beautiful white doves in the sky. Thank you for the nice headstone. I've come to understand about love and the connection of people with Angels on earth, those who helped me. But the most special angel I have, Mom, is you. It always was.

Kathy:	Did you ever see the angel who came to the hospital and told us what was wrong with you?
Brian: .	No, I haven't seen him yet, but I've learned that Angels can come and help families. They appear and then go when their work is done. Someday I'd like to help people too, but right now I have lots to learn. Later on I want to help children—autistic children, and children with speech problems, and sick children. I gave my clothes and my CDs to my friends.
Kathy:	Is there anything special you want me to do?
Brian:	Everything you do is special. I'd like you to look after yourself, laugh and smile again like you used to, take a trip, just take some time for you. See the beauty of the world; try to see past what happened to me. Just enjoy the beauty around you.
Kathy:	Did you like what we did for your funeral?
Brian:	I wasn't there any more. I was already gone from my body. It doesn't matter what you do at funerals, it's more for you, the living, than for me. Everything is perfect here and love is everywhere. What counts is the years of love you gave me, it was so pure and beautiful. It's because of your love I made it through. Many times, it didn't appear to help, but your love brought me through some of the darkest times of my life.
Kathy:	Do you like the presents I leave for you in your room?
Nadine:	Brian is laughing.
Brian:	Mom, you worry too much. You have to let go a little. As you let go, I can do more here. I love my room. I go through the whole house. I'm drawn by your energy. It's your energy that I go to. Material things mean nothing to me now. It's who you are and what you do on earth that's important. That's what you take with you to Heaven. I'm drawn to you, Mom, not to material things. Like when you think of me, and that you remember what I liked; that brings us together.

Kathy:	What caused your death? Was it because of the creatine you took in Youth Custody?
Brian:	No, Mom and it's not important any more. Don't sue the Juvenile Justice System it won't bring me back. It's too hard on you and brings back negative energy. It will only drag up bad memories. Concentrate on moving forward. Mom, there are beautiful flowers where I am. Remember I love you, Mom and take care of yourself for me.

With that last message, my hour was up and the tape stopped. It seemed so simple yet so strange to be taping a conversation with my deceased son. Nadine placed a tape recorder beside her chair at the start of our session and as we spoke it was recorded. The only sad part was that at no time could I hear my son's voice only that of Nadine and myself.

I could have talked forever and I hated to leave. I said goodbye, and left Nadine's house. I wished I could have more, but I also knew I had received lots in such a short time and Brian was right, I did need to let go a little. He deserved a chance to do the things important to his spirit now.

I clutched the tape as I walked out to the car; it was as if this tape was Brian. It took me a whole year before I had the nerve to listen to it so that I might write this chapter. But, I'm glad I did listen to the tape again. The time is right now, and I understand much more now than I did when I went to Nadine, of what Brian was telling me about life on earth and life after death.

After my visit with Nadine, I could think of nothing else but seeing Brian again. All my conversations inevitably led right back to my main subject, Brian. How I could reach him, signs I had received from him, readings I had with psychics and books I was reading on life after death. I tried to learn to meditate but my mind was going in too many directions at once. I sometimes felt like a failure. I didn't understand why I couldn't meditate and reach my own son, for books made it sound so easy. The question now was, "Where do I go from here?"

What Next: Can I Rebuild My Life?

What Next:
Can I rebuild my Life

My first book was finished and ready for my family in time for Christmas, 1999. I met this deadline by self-publishing *Brian's World: Can't You See What I See,"* with the help of a friend who owns a franchised photocopying business. I started telling people about *Brian's World* and before long, I was actually getting requests from friends and acquaintances to purchase a copy of the book. This was more than I could have ever dreamed of but I felt it was a special kind of legacy—one from me to my youngest child, Brian, and also one from Brian to his mom.

Now I knew for certain that his life had a purpose and I was helping with that purpose. I felt that by telling Brian's story I would be able to help other Disabled Youth and their families. I also felt *Brian's World* could reach many of the street kids. It was for many young adults like Brian—their story. They could relate and I hoped I could bring some peace, understanding and sense of self-worth back to their lives.

Next, I managed to complete and edit the video of Brian's life. That was a very long and extremely emotional undertaking. I had to go through some twenty photograph albums of Brian's pictures and view over fifteen VHS tapes containing video footage of Brian from birth until just before his death. Looking at all those pictures and video tapes made me wish even more that Brian was still with me. I'd find my mind playing tricks on me as I visualized Brian still alive—just away at school for a little while.

I began to wait for signs at every corner. I began checking the phone in his room more often just to see if he was on the other end. I'd look at all the young dark-haired boys we passed in our car in case one of them was my son trying to find his way home to me. I checked my telephone and voice mail for a message from Brian. I even tried, on an almost daily basis, to meditate. I begged Brian to give me more signs.

I started writing to psychics who had written books which I had read, but those such as James Van Praagh and Rosemary Altea were no longer able to give private readings. I continued to read more books and learn all I could about life after death. I even thought about going to grief counseling again.

I did try some grief counseling with a friend who is a counselor. I found it very difficult to answer her questions as they were personal and she is a close friend so I made only one visit. I asked Ian about his company's counseling service. His answer was always the same. "We go to Compassionate Friends, don't you think that is enough?" Once I openly told him that I wanted more than Compassionate Friends, but he replied, "We're doing fine, and we certainly don't need a counselor to tell us how to live life without Brian."

One memorable day I took a break from the book, the video, and life. I went to lunch with Brian's friend, Jessica. She had called to say she had something she wanted to give me and to ask me to meet her for lunch. When we met, I was excited to learn that the gift she had for me was in the form of the text of the lyrics to a song—a song Brian had dedicated to me when he was in Youth Custody in January, 1998. The song was called "*Mama*" by a group called "Boys to Men".

This song helped to settle my life for a little while. It made me realize that Brian had always loved me and that he understood how important he was to me. Now I knew I had been just as important to him. The only thing lacking was for me to have some grief counseling so that I could begin a new way of relating to life without my youngest son. I now had to learn to understand and accept that though I couldn't physically see Brian, he would always be there to talk to me and to guide me, if I would only give him the chance.

The roles were now reversed. Brian no longer needed me to guide his life, but I needed him to guide mine. I spent hours talking to my son and trying to get to know him as a free spirit, an angel who was there for me whenever I needed him. It took me many months to learn that I didn't need a sign from Brian every day or every month to know he was there. All I really needed was to have faith in God, faith in my son, and some counseling. In June 2000 my husband relented and said, "If you feel you need counseling then get it."

I did, and found it to be successful in releasing my fears and angers. It was a perfect way to get to know my innermost self as I rid my mind of blame for something that was completely beyond my control. Grief counseling taught me that there is a life for me beyond the death of my child. All I need do is look towards those loved ones who are living and who are near to know that I am still needed and loved. Life does continue without Brian. I know that I will be able to have a long, useful, happy life even if my Brian can no longer be physically here with me.

Today I try not to weep over the loss of my beautiful son but rather to say, "Thank you." Now I thank God every night and morning and many times in between for the gift of my son. Through his short life and his untimely death, Brian has given me much. He taught me about life, about myself and about love. He gave me the gift of me, allowing me to be myself, to do what I have loved to do since I was very young—to write. And what better to be my first writings than the story of my son and the pain of losing that son. I can honestly say with a happy heart, "Yes Kathy, there is life after Brian."

Signs: Learning Not To Expect Lightening Bolts

For me just learning to see the beauty that surrounds
my world is a sign of love from my son.

Signs: Learning not to Expect Lightening Bolts

My life was taking shape again, or so I hoped. It was now late October 1999, and *Brian's World* was in the printer's hands. The background music for the video about Brian's life was now complete, thanks to Jessica and her gift of the final song on the video *"Mama"*. I was ready to take a look at my life and move on. The only task remaining was to assemble the final selection of video and photographic material and deliver this material to Pro Video—the company which would put together the presentation which would become a special Christmas gift to my family.

Until this time I had wished—no, begged—for signs from Brian. Big electrifying signs. I wanted to see Brian, to touch him—even to hear his voice. I looked for signs everywhere, and I thought everything was a sign.

I had read in one book that all faith, all religions and all spiritual disciplines are interrelated; all are intertwined in the workings of our universe. This same book also spoke of the importance of confession to the soul and to the spirit. I had stopped going to confession in my early twenties. I had heard that it wasn't important, that you could tell God your sins yourself, that you didn't need confession unless you committed a really terrible sin. But now I once again understood the importance of confession in the Catholic faith. So, after thirty years, I again started going to confession.

The question I most needed to have answered was, "Is looking for and asking for signs a sin?"

Father Michael really helped me. "You won't get signs every day or every week," he explained. "And after a while, when you are ready, you won't get any more signs. And remember, signs don't come as lightening bolts. They are very subtle, and meant for the person who sees them. They won't come to you in a crowd of people where you all jump up and scream, 'Glory be! We just got another sign!' The love between a mother and her son is very strong, and that love doesn't leave in death. But just because someone else says they got a sign, and you did not get one doesn't mean you loved, or were loved, any less. It just means that you didn't know it was a sign when you got it. Not everyone will know when they receive a sign, and not all signs are immediate. Signs come when we need them to let us know our loved ones are still with us, and will continue to be with us whenever we need them."

Father Michael's talk really gave me a lot to think about. Now, along with all the books I had been reading, I had some serious thinking to do. In the year and a half since the death of my son, I had learned a lot about myself, life, love and my faith.

During this time of coming to terms and of recognition, I looked back over the many things I felt and did during the saddest time in my life. While reflecting on the events of those eighteen months, my understanding of signs, fantasies and just plain longing for my son's return came full circle. I could better distinguish the realities of my life.

The reality was that my youngest son is dead. I know that no amount of prayers or tears or miracles will lead to his return to me. I am able to accept that purchasing gifts for Brian means nothing to him now. Material things have no meaning for him in Heaven, for there he has everything he needs and his only wants are to see me happy again and for me in turn to rejoice in his good fortune in being among God's chosen ones.

What Brian is able to receive and hear are my prayers for him. He can feel the love I have for him; he can send his love to me by means of subtle signs. He can heighten my awareness of the beauty of the world around me; he can even send me rainbows of love. But a roomful of his belongings is just material possessions which are no longer needed by him. I can now accept that these material things are for my benefit, not his. I can now accept that these things make me feel good. Brian is a spirit and all his needs are met. He's happy when I laugh and sad when I cry and I know he's in a much better place than I am. Neither hurt nor anger will ever come his way again.

Brian no longer needs either earthly possessions or his earthly body. He is no longer ill; nor is he addicted to poisonous substances. He's fine; he is an angel who is always with me. He protects me and watches out for me and intercedes with God on my behalf.

At first, I wanted signs. I would ask Brian to visit me; to take my hand; to let me see his face; or to let me hear his voice when I picked up the phone. I wanted him to give me signs each minute of every day. In the beginning I thought that such signs would change the outcome for me, would bring my son back—or at the very least, bring him closer to me. I've learned a great deal since those early days of my grief.

During the past year and a half, I have received many signs from Brian. Most were subtle and meant for me alone. I have learned to love these signs and to accept them when they are sent to me. One very significant sign was in the form of the ring which Brian sent to me in June 1999. I am grateful for that gift which helped our entire family and Brian's friends to know and understand that Brian is still watching over us all.

On July 9, 2000, another sign of great significance was seen by ten of Brian's friends, by his dad, and by myself. On that day, we hosted a poolside party for staff and residents of the local Safe House, and also for some of Brian's friends. A number of us were standing near the pool trying to decide which part of Brian's memorial garden would make the best setting for a group photograph. As we looked across the pool towards Brian's garden, an osprey swooped from nowhere and hovered a few feet above our heads. With his head bent toward our group, he hovered and looked from one to another of us, as if he wanted to take one more look at his friends. While the bird hovered in this way, a former staff member from the Safe House asked, "Do you feel that? I feel Brian's presence with us at this very moment."

We all agreed that we felt something, and as we gazed upwards, the bird took one last darting look and, as quickly as he had come, was gone. We stood awe-struck as he flew upwards, across the river, and out of sight. For a few moments, no one broke the hushed silence—then all of us tried to be heard at once. It was a very special moment which I will remember the rest of my life.

Earlier that same day, while attending Mass at Holy Family Church, I looked up, as I often do, to the window above the altar, praying for just a glimpse of Brian. I was given that glimpse. The experience was so intense that I couldn't move. I wanted to grab Ian's arm and say. "Do you see him too, or am I actually losing my mind?" But I was paralyzed. I'm sure my face must have shown signs of my awe and confusion. I remember the details so vividly. This event took place just before the congregation knelt to say the Eucharistic Prayer. I could hear what was going on around me in the church, but I couldn't move for fear I would lose sight of Brian. I willed myself to look away from the window for a second. I had to make sure I was not dreaming. When I looked back, he was still there. It was only Brian's face that I saw—a profile drawn in the clouds and looking straight before him. I remember kneeling and thinking, "I can't look away, or he'll be gone."

A few seconds later Father said, "We'll use Eucharistic Prayer Number Two for children."

I knew I had to bow my head to pray and I knew that when I raised it again, Brian would be gone. And that is exactly what happened. There was no cloud formation left to be seen through the window, not even a distortion of what I had seen remained. There was only a clear blue sky, and Brian's face too had vanished. I wished I had had a camera with me to capture that image of my son, but that image was meant for me, and for me alone. I will cherish its memory.

Both Ian and I have been given many other subtle signs from our son. Let me tell you about just a few. The Compassionate Friends group to which we belong meets on the first Thursday of each month and it was at the meeting in March, 2000 that Ian mentioned for the first time that he missed Brian. This was a real breakthrough for my husband; for over a year I had waited to hear him say this.

On the morning of the following Saturday as Ian and I went outside to work in the yard, the telephone rang. It was our daughter Rebecca calling and as I talked to her, Ian stood by the door of the house to let out the dogs. All of a sudden, Ian began pointing and gasping, but not saying anything.

"What's wrong?" I asked as my husband waved his hands and pointed, still unable to speak. At the other end of the telephone line Rebecca was asking, "What's wrong, Mom?" Then I saw why Ian was waving. He pointed above his head to where a large eagle hovered within reach. Ian later said he was so nervous that he couldn't speak. The eagle actually looked as if it were about to grab my husband's hat. Had Ian not been waving his arms so frantically, I'm sure the bird would have seized the hat.

I explained to Rebecca what was going on so that she would know we were both OK. When I was able to think clearly, I said "Ian, I think that was Brian. He probably would have grabbed your hat had you not been flapping your arms so wildly. I think he wanted to let you know he was glad you still think about him and miss him, because he still thinks about you and misses you. And wouldn't that be just like our Brian to play a trick like grabbing your hat and flying off with it!"

In October 1999, while I was working on the video of the story of Brian's life I would spend hours each day seated in front of the video machine reviewing tape after tape of Brian's growing up. And I would spend further hours examining photograph albums by the dozen as I searched for just the right pictures to complete the video. Many times the pain would be too great. I would switch off the machine, close the albums and sit motionless, staring, and sometimes weeping. On most of these occasions, I would smell a faint hint of vanilla in the air. The first time this happened I got up and looked around the room to make sure I hadn't left a candle burning somewhere. I even checked to see if the scent were not coming from the unlit candle across the room from me. The scent did not seem to come from any particular source; rather, it just wafted past me on those saddest of moments. I came to think of it as Brian's way of letting me know that he was near me always, and of reminding me not to cry for him for he was happy—happier than he had been throughout most of his difficult life. Brian knew that I loved the scent of vanilla and often had many vanilla candles burning throughout our home in Prince Albert. I remember him asking me, "Don't you ever get sick of that smell?"

And I answered, "No. It is a very beautiful scent.

There was a day in spring 1999, when Ian and I worked in the yard; a chilling wind was blowing and I felt both cold and sad. Ian went round the corner to work and I stood sheltered from the wind by the garage. I was half daydreaming about Brian and about how our lives used to be when all of a sudden I heard what I thought was Ian's voice calling my name. The sound seemed to come from far away but I heard it very distinctly. At first I heard, "Kathy." Then, as I came out of my daydream, I heard my name being called several times. It was being said in the same tone Brian would use when he was having difficulty in getting my attention. It sounded like,

"Kathy…Ka-a-athy…Ka-a-ath-th-thy-y-y."

I came to completely and started towards Ian who was still at the other side of the yard. When I reached him I asked, "Did you call me?"

He looked at me strangely. "No, I didn't call you."

"I distinctly heard my name being called three times," I continued.

Ian shook his head: "You must be hearing things."

"No," I answered quietly. "No…I distinctly heard my name being called three times in the same way Brian used to call me when I wasn't paying attention to him. I think Brian was just saying 'Hello.' "

"Maybe he was," said Ian. "Who knows, maybe he was…But I do need your help now that you are out here!"

In April 2000 we were repairing a stretch of riverbank and clearing some brush we had cut the previous fall. It was a hard job and Ian and I both grew tired and cranky. With the job only half done, Ian suddenly announced that he had to go to the office for an hour or so. I was furious because he knew that if we did not finish burning the brush piles that weekend we would have to hire a truck to haul them away. My husband knew I was upset with him and said, "Why don't you take a break while I'm gone, and I'll help you finish when I get back. There's something I have to take care of at the office and I almost forgot about it."

I just looked at him and kept on working, knowing full well that the job was too big for me to finish on my own. I no longer seemed to have the physical strength I used to have before we lost Brian. So, as I continued throwing brush-wood from the riverbank, I began to feel sorry for myself. As I picked up one fairly heavy and awkward branch I lost my balance and almost fell from the ledge with the log. I still do not know what saved me, but I did not fall and neither was I hurt. I began to weep; the tears just started flowing and would not stop. I wondered why it seemed I always had to be alone. Why did I have to lose Brian? I could always count on Brian being there for me. Just then, for no obvious reason, I felt compelled to lift my head from between my hands and look upward. There, above me, a powerful eagle soared. As I watched, the eagle did a beautiful and graceful dance against the sky and I thought, "you're right, Brian. I'm not alone. I will never be alone, for all I have to do is think of you and you'll be here."

I thanked Brian for this reminder that he was always with me and was then able to continue my work in an atmosphere of peace and tranquility.

There have been many other little signs from Brian, such as the light from his special candle dancing when it is lit. On occasion, I have lit several candles next to Brian's special candle, but always his is the only one whose flame dances. Some days it dances more than others do; and some days it hardly dances at all. But most times that special candle will dance all evening—a constant reminder that Brian's spirit is with us, always.

In May 2000 two events occurred which I believe were Brian's special ways of trying to communicate with me. On a Wednesday morning early in May, our bedside telephone rang at about 7:30. Ian was getting ready to go to work and, thinking my friend or my daughter might be phoning, I lifted the receiver. The sound coming from the phone was distorted by static electricity, but through the crackling interference, I could clearly hear a heart beating. No voices; no greeting; no conversation; just the sound of a steady heartbeat. I listened to that heartbeat, saying "Hello" periodically, for about a minute-and-a-half.

Ian heard my repeated "hellos" and came back into the room asking, "Who's on the phone?" I explained that, at first, I thought it might be Rebecca having an ultrasound examination and letting me hear the baby's heartbeat.

"But there is still no one on the line," I said. "All I can hear is a heartbeat; I'm sure that's what it is."

Ian then took the phone and listened. He too said "Hello" into the handset. Turning to me he said, "This is strange. It sounds like a heartbeat."

I ran downstairs to check the information in our message manager. It identified the call as being out of area and gave no other details. I ran back up the stairs to tell Ian, and with the full intention of listening a while longer. As I relayed the "out of area" message to him, Ian said, "It must be a wrong number," and put down the receiver before I could seize it from his hand. When I picked up the phone again, I heard only a dial tone. I always felt that the heartbeat was Brian's and that he was trying to reach me.

About two weeks later, Ian was working late at the office and I sat down to watch television. When I turned on the set, there was no picture—only snow; but as I looked at the screen I easily distinguished a face through the snow. It resembled Brian's face. As I studied the picture, I noticed that there was indeed a program taking place behind the snow; I could see people moving about in a room, and there were some outdoor scenes—although these were ever-so-faint. But the image of Brian's face was so distinct that I could not take my gaze from the television screen for nearly two hours.

"What are you watching?" asked Ian when he came home. I explained that when I had turned on the set the screen had looked like that, and that I was sure it was Brian trying to communicate with me. Ian quickly stepped towards the television.

"Let me see if I can get something to come through on that screen for you." With these words, he changed the channel and the TV was working again. Who really knows why these mysterious things happen? But for my part, I choose to think of them as messages from my son in Heaven.

I'll leave you with my most recent signs from Brian which started on December 9 and December 24, 2000. In November, Ian and I had gone to Florida to vacation with our oldest son, Michael. During the trip, I mentioned to Ian that I would like a pinky mother's ring as a Christmas gift, and while on holiday we looked at the selection offered in a few jewelry stores. When I returned home, I got busy writing, for I wanted to enter stories in the annual Christmas Story contest run by our local newspapers. One of the stories I wrote was about my Christmas Dream and told how my special Christmas dream was that there would be a gift under the tree on Christmas morning addressed: "To Mom with love. Your son," and as I turned round, there would be Brian smiling back at me. I entered the contest and forgot all about the story—until December 9th. On that afternoon, Ian and I decided to clean the garage to make room for a new dog I was getting after Christmas. As I cleared off our catchall table, something glittery caught my attention. I picked it up and couldn't believe my eyes. It was a gold pinky ring in my size. The ring was set with a small diamond, and from the diamond hung a gold topaz, the birthstone for November—Brian's birth month. Neither Ian nor I could believe what we saw, but right away we both thought that it was a gift from Brian.

The next morning was December 10th and as I was getting ready for church, Ian hollered up from the kitchen, "Kathy, look out the window! Hurry!"

I did as Ian asked and could hardly contain my excitement for, circling above our yard were two of the largest bald eagles I have ever seen. One flew away suddenly, but the larger of the two flew to a tree on the lawn and perched there. His wingspan must have been at least six feet but as he settled onto a branch, he looked directly towards our house and directly at me as I peered at him through the bedroom window. The eagle sat there for at least twenty minutes, gazing at our home. Desperately, I tried to get my camera to work, but the batteries had died only the day before. I turned to ask Ian a question and, when we looked again towards the tree, the eagle had gone. We looked out at the sky, searching, but nowhere was the eagle to be seen. And then I remembered my Christmas story, and as I smiled at Ian, holding out the hand which wore the pinky ring, I repeated the words from my story: "As I turned around he was smiling back at me."

I will always believe the ring was from Brian and the eagle was Brian smiling back at me saying. "Have a Merry Christmas, Mom; and remember I'm with you always. All you have to do is think of me and I'll be there."

Just when my life was getting back on track, a child who attended my church died. I decided to help out with the funeral lunch and thus try to give back some of the kindness given to me at the time of my own son's funeral. I had the strength to help prepare the lunch; I had the strength to attend the funeral mass; and at the end of this difficult experience I thought, "You made it through, my friend. You're on your way to complete healing." And as I turned around, I saw the little casket being wheeled out of the church–and I broke down.

Fortunately, my friend Carol from Compassionate Friends was there to comfort me. We sat awhile and talked softly and Carol's quiet words reassured me:

"Take your time and keep in mind that the second year can be more difficult than the first to endure."

After the shocking realization that I was not completely healed of my grief, I consulted yet another spiritual medium that a friend had recommended to me. The medium, whose name is John, is of very high repute. John told me many things which he said my son was relaying to him, but two messages from Brian were to me of outstanding importance.

"I've moved on, Mom, but you're still in the same place. It was my time to die. An angel came and told me it was my time, and nothing you could have done would have changed the outcome." He continued, "But there is a message I would like you to convey in your new book, *Life After Brian*, and that is, 'There is a life after death.' Let people know that you have seen me and that I am fine. I am merely doing God's work now."

Then, through John, Brian gave me a set of very specific instructions.

"Before you go to bed tonight, turn on the dim light over the bed and sit and look into the mirror of your bureau. I will appear to you tonight. You will see that I am fine. Please trust me. It will take lots of energy and I will need to use some of your energy too, but we can do this and then you must let people know that you saw me and that I am fine."

That night I retired to my room at about eleven o'clock. As instructed, I turned out the light that lit my room but dimly, sat on the side of my bed, and looked into the mirror. At first I was very frightened and kept turning my head away; then I became anxious to look. As I gazed into the mirror, my own image faded to be replaced by that of my son's face. Several times I looked away, and when I looked back and asked, Brian would again show his face in place of mine in the mirror. Neither of us spoke, but mentally I encouraged him to try harder for, at first, all I saw were his eyes. Then his nose appeared, and finally his whole face appeared in place of mine in the mirror. This went on for about forty minutes then in my mind I said, "Thank you Brian for now I know you are fine. I will tell people that there is a life after death, but for now you are weakening and I am very tired. Remember I love you, goodbye for now." At that instant Brian's image disappeared and the reflection of my own face returned to the mirror.

To those who ask me how I am able to go on after the death of my child I answer: "I'm no stronger than any other person. But now I do understand that I have a commitment to life, to my children, to my husband and to God. So I do the best I can to fulfill these commitments—'one day at a time'."

As I was ready to bring this book to a close, Brian gave me one last gift. I feel it may be my last visit from him for a while, but I'm OK with that knowledge now. It was on December 24, 2000—the morning of Christmas Eve and a Sunday. We were spending Christmas in Prince Albert with Rebecca and her family.

Now, because it was Sunday there would be the regular Sunday morning Mass, and because it was Christmas Eve there would also be the annual Christmas Eve Mass. I wanted to attend both and I asked my daughter, eldest son, husband and grandchildren. They all said the same thing:

"You want me to go to church twice in one day?"

When I answered, "Yes," they all replied,
"No!"
Then my dad spoke up, "I'll go to Mass with you."

Ian drove dad and me to St. Joseph's Church for Sunday Mass. This is the church we attended all through Brian's childhood. This is the church in which Brian made his First Holy Communion and Confirmation, and where he served as altar boy nearly every Sunday, not so many years ago.

As we entered the church I was greeted and hugged by our Deacon a former neighbour. It gave me such a warm feeling to be back in this familiar round church with its domed roof and soft-beige brick walls, and its poignant memories of Brian as a child.

When it was time to recite the Lord's Prayer the congregation all took hands, which was the usual practice in St. Joseph's. In our pew there was only my dad and myself, so we took each other's and each of us stretched our free hand out as if to clasp another, imaginary hand. This is the common practice when no one is beside you. As I began to say the Lord's Prayer I felt someone take my out-stretched hand, lowering it as they did so. I turned to see who was beside me; I blinked and looked again. There was no one there. Yet I felt someone hold my hand. Then I smiled to myself as my mind whispered, "Hello, Brian."

I was once again reminded of those special Sundays only a few short years ago at this same church. I would feel someone take my hand and turn to find Brian standing beside me, his hand in mine, as he mouthed the words, "I made it Mom." To date, the presence of Brian beside me on December 24, 2000 was my last sign from him._

But the holiday season was perfect. My parents; Michael and Becky and her family; Ian and Brian; all were celebrating the holidays with me. What could be more special than that!

Over the course of the two years following my son's death, I had come to appreciate and understand the meaning of the word "sign." I know that not everything I see is a sign. I certainly know that every time I see a butterfly flutter-ing in Brian's memorial garden, or that each time the eagle soars nearby it isn't Brian—or even a sign from Brian. But what I have learned is that signs are what you want them to be, what you feel in your heart, what reminds you of your loved one. When I see the eagle soar, I stop whatever I am doing and remember. I remember the fun Brian and I had and the love we shared. I remember that he was and always will be a free spirit and, like the eagle, he can now soar to the greatest heights. I know that Brian doesn't paint the rainbows or the beautiful sunsets for me to see, but they remind me of how he loved the world we lived in.

I know he doesn't make my flowers grow to exceptional height in his garden, but watching those flowers grow and bloom and watching so many tiny living creatures visit his garden remind me of Brian, and remind me of the years I spent watching him grow and turn into the fine young man he wanted to be. The creatures always remind me of Brian's words, and I can still hear him today as he would say, "Mom, don't step on that ant. What did it ever do to you? He has a right to live too, you know. And what if his mom is looking for him, and can't find him? She'll be lonesome too."

And he was so right; for we do all have a purpose.

Signs for me mean many things, and to the lives of each one of us, they can bring a different meaning. But one thing is certain, we all have to deal with the death of our children or other loved ones in our own way and in our own time. Some of us do need signs to help us cope; others need only time. There is no right or wrong way to grieve for we are all individual in our beliefs and in how we conduct our lives. To all who have experienced loss, remember the grief is ours alone to bear. And to those who ask me why I talk of signs when you have seen none I say, "Each in his own time, each in her own way." You may already have received a sign—a sign so subtle that only the sender knows it happened.

I have a good friend who said to me, "Kathy, you know the signs aren't real. When you die you go to Heaven and you are happy. You don't know sadness any more, nor do you know pain. So how can someone from a wonderful place like that see your need for a sign? It just doesn't happen. When my child passed away I never got any signs, nor did I look for any. I just understood that my child was at peace with God in a much better place."

A few moments later when she was telling me of the death of her mother, she explained how, shortly after her mother had died, she found herself in a grocery store with her daughter. She said that she and her daughter both smelt perfume, the type of perfume they associated with her mom. She said that it lasted only moments and then was gone. She continued by saying that she and her daughter both thought it strange and then dismissed it from their minds.

"That was a sign from your mother," I said. "She gave you a sign that she was OK."

My friend said that she had never before thought of it as a sign as she doesn't believe in signs. This is what I mean when I say you may have received a sign without recognizing its significance at the time. For most signs are subtle and meant for you and you alone. Very few hit us like lightening bolts.

I wrote the following poem in memory of Brian in October 2000, on the second anniversary of his death.

I Know You Are There

Each morning I lie awake as I listen
To the birds as they sing your sweet songs
When I step into the crisp morning air
I feel your cool breath and I know you are there
I envision you out fishing where the river runs by
I feel your embrace as the sun warms where I lie
I see your tears of joy in the dew and the mist
After each storm, you send me a rainbow above in the sky
Reminding me my treasure is the beauty nearby
As a breeze blows through my hair
You whisper "I miss you," and I know you are there
And when the wind rustles through the trees
You add, "Always remember me, please"
The mountains above all echo your love
I watch in awe as the eagle soars up above
I blink as I look for there on his wing
I see you flying so at peace and so free
I remember your beauty and your favorite pie
As I look up at the glorious sunset sky
Then in the clouds so high and so soft
I watch as you rest just floating aloft
You're still beside me wherever I go
I see your face in each flower I grow
I watch as a butterfly, hornet, and bee
Spread your love to each living thing they see
I feel your presence in church as I kneel down to pray
I watch you dance in the candle flame day after day
I see your sweet smile as I look toward the moon
I long for the day we'll be together, I wish it were soon
I've seen your dancing eyes and your face.
I've seen your smile so warm and so bright

Right there in my mirror through the pale night light
Because of these things and so many more
I feel it in my heart, I know you are there
I whisper, "I love you," as I bow my head in prayer
And as I close my eyes at the end of each day
I thank you for showing me the way
Then I smile as I drift off to the land of dreams
Where I visit you so happy, so alive, so keen
My dreams are of you my angel, my guiding light
So until we meet again in Heavenly delight
I send you my love, my hugs, and my kisses
Then I see you smile as you wave with all your might
As I drift off I hear, "Remember, I love you. Good-night."

I Bear The Bitter Grief—One Day At A Time

I Bear the Bitter Grief—One Day at a Time

Holidays come and go every year just as they always did but they are no longer the same for me. I must remind myself often that the calendar marks not Christmas the commercial hullabaloo but Christ's Mass, the celebration of the birth of our Saviour. The commercial aspects are all man-made for our own selfish enjoyment. I often wonder now what the holidays would be like if Christmas were again what it was meant to be—a celebration of the birth of Jesus. Would children go to mass with their parents then return home and say a few prayers for our Saviour? Would they spend the day in silent prayer and feasting over the joy of the birth of Christ?

How differently I might have done things had I known the life of my youngest son would be so short and that the years we would have together would be thus numbered. I think I would have taught him more about prayer and the true meaning of the holiday celebrations. But he knew, he always knew for his faith was steadfast and his belief strong. I believe he was prepared for his death, much more so than I.

So where to go from here? What to do with the rest of my life? How does one's life continue after the death of a child? It's all up to the individual. There is no magical point in time when grief ends or sorrow melts completely from the heart. The pain may lessen, but it is unlikely that it will vanish.

I will never again see our youngest son smile, or hear him laugh, or listen to one of his oh-so-important "I need" phone calls. Fortunately, I have those memories etched in my heart and mind. I once worried that I may eventually forget the sound of his voice or the way he smiled at me but I now realize that these are mine to keep forever, for they are the special gifts my son left to me. I do not believe a day will go by that I don't remember Brian in some way. With time he may not be the only person I think of, but his memory will always be just a thought away.

I got through the second anniversary of Brian's death, and what would have been his twenty-first birthday on November 14th, but just around the corner there is Christmas, and beyond that another new year without him. All the tomorrows he left without seeing sadden me. Yet, I know they weren't meant to be in his destiny. We are fortunate to have enjoyed and loved such a very special child as Brian for even a little while.

There will be many more birthdays and holidays when Brian will be remembered and missed. I often wonder how I can celebrate without Brian, but I do. We've changed our holiday traditions, and I get through with the help of family and friends who have made changes and adjustments that allow me space to cope with my loss.

On October 25 1999, we began to observe new customs in memory of our son, for we wanted to remember Brian in a way best for our family. Ian and I attend a special mass said for Brian on the anniversary of his death. We purchase a single white rose and some balloons and go quietly together to the cemetery. We place the rose on our son's grave then, after a few silent moments; we release the balloons to freedom and watch as they race through the clouds and to our son in Heaven.

We wish Brian would wave and say, "Thank you for the balloons. They're beautiful." In my mind and in my heart I see him wave and whisper, "Thanks, Mom. I love you lots." I know Brian retrieves the balloons because as we stand, watching them rise through the clouds, the sky comes alive with astonishing color. The beauty of the sky is our "Thank you" from Brian. As we leave the cemetery a wave of inner peace comes over me reminding me that I need not worry—our Brian is fine.

To celebrate Brian's birthday we plant an evergreen tree in our yard; we will plant a new tree each year on his birthday for as long as we are able. The tree is significant because of Brian's love of the forest and his interest in preserving the earth. In Memory Of Brian, we take a birthday cake to the local Safe House. I light his special candle, wishing for him eternal peace and happiness, and other members of our family who live out of town also light a candle in Brian's memory. We try to celebrate Brian's life—not mourn his death. I know that this is what he wants.

Christmas is a particularly difficult time because it was a special season for Brian and I. We both loved the holiday, the decorations, all the baked goodies—and Brian so enjoyed gifts. As it turned out the worrying was worse than the actual day, thanks to our wonderful daughter who took charge. She knows just what we need. We now go to Rebecca's home; she does all the decorating and baking and we enjoy our highly personable son-in-law and our beloved grand-children. At first, I did not want to spend Christmas at my daughter's but now I look forward to it. Our oldest son Michael has even made arrangements to come home for the holidays and how grateful we are to have him with us once again.

We take Brian's special candle to Rebecca's house where it burns throughout the holiday. In the window of our own home, there is an angel holding a candle and with a lighted candle on each side of her. This angel display is powered by electricity; the two candles have burned continuously since the first anniversary of Brian's death and will continue to burn as long as I live. We have decided not to have a Christmas tree inside our home for the present, but we decorate Brian's birthday tree that grows by our front steps.

One of the most important new traditions we now have to help us cope with the holiday season is attending the Compassionate Friends Candle Lighting service. This heart-warming occasion is a non-denominational service and is held in memory of all our lost children. Even with these newly established family traditions to console and strengthen me, I still have sad days and happy days, but the changes have helped to lessen the sorrow so that I can enjoy my living children while remembering my deceased son.

Throughout the year, we do different things in Brian's memory. At Christmas and Easter, we take gifts of traditional holiday fare to the local Safe House in Brian's name. During the summer, there is a barbecue and pool party held at our home for the local Safe House when all the street kids are welcome to join us. I pray that in some small way my son's death will help touch another child's life with a second chance.

I've spent the last two years searching to find a place I was unwittingly looking for all my life. I sought a life filled with happiness and contentment, a life I could call mine and feel good about living. The death of my son brought me to the realization that though I thought I hadn't found whatever it was I sought, it had been there all along. To grasp it and make it mine I only had to reach out. It was the love of my family and friends; the beauty of the world we live in; the faith I've practiced all my life but never really knew or understood. It was all there at arm's length, but it took the death of my son to show me what had been mine all along.

The second year after Brian's death seemed to be much harder to bear than the twelve months immediately following my loss. The days seemed to drag by in loneliness as I turned all of my thoughts to the child I had lost and waited for signs. At times it seemed I forgot those who lived and needed me. It took me nearly two long years to come to terms with the fact that the death of my son didn't happen to me alone; it happened to our whole family, and to his many good and close friends who all miss him as much as I do.

Writing this book was extremely painful and it has taken the better part of the last two years to complete the task. The truth is, I kept making excuses not to write, so I wouldn't have to face the finality of the situation. I wanted to live in the past and forget there must be a future.

By completing the book, I have at last found the answers I had been seeking throughout my adult life. I have within me the power to control my own destiny. I helped create the world that surrounds me, be it happy or sad. All my life I looked for happiness; I wanted to belong and to be needed. I wanted acceptance and approval to be me—not what people expected me to be.

I found all of these in my relationship with Brian. Because Brian was a sickly child from birth, I devoted all my attentions to his health and happiness. Because of the ten-year age difference between Brian and his siblings, I had many hours to spend with him. I created a world around Brian where I was needed and loved. I was in a place where I thought I would always belong. Then Brian died, and in one brief moment, all was changed. Brian was gone and along with him my life and my identity. I thought I could never be happy again. I felt alone and angry. I *knew* no one else needed me or loved me as much as Brian had. I was wrong, of course. My other children, my grandchildren and my husband all need me. My parents, siblings and friends all need me too. But I'd become so wrapped up in my world with Brian and then my loss of him, that I forgot to live.

To compensate for my loss I tried to keep Brian alive. By doing that, I was able to make life bearable for me. For nearly two years, I continued to inhabit a world in which Brian was still alive. I even turned our home into a shrine for him. I rationalized that to let Brian die would be to lose me.

I have learned about many of my fears and angers with the help of my counselor, but it was my friend Dorothy who gave me the knowledge to understand my life. She put Brian's death in perspective for me. Dorothy's young son had died in August 1999. Late in July 2000, we two sat at my kitchen table talking about the pain of losing our respective sons. We were both crying, something neither of us does well or often.

We each spoke about the struggle to cope with the death of a son, about our highs, our lows, and how difficult and unfair life seemed. I confided to Dorothy that I just didn't seem to care about life anymore. That even getting out of bed was a chore. I told her that there was no longer anyone who needed me. I went on to explain how Brian had always needed me and how alone I'd felt since his death. I told Dorothy how strange it seemed that everyone's life had gone on while mine stood still. I had even noticed that Brian's friends had stopped going to the cemetery to visit him as frequently as they once had and the silly innocent gifts they left there seemed to be getting fewer and fewer. It seemed that no one understood how I felt.

We had been speaking for about an hour when Dorothy said something that has given me a new perspective on a very unhappy life.

"Kathy," she said, "I don't think Brian needed you as much as you need him. You lived your life through Brian, so when he died you died too. Don't you see? Brian had to die so you could live. If Brian had lived, you would not have had a life; you would have continued living his life for him until there was no life left for either of you. But in the aftermath of Brian's death, you're not letting him die. You need to give him that gift, let him rest in peace. Let him do whatever it is he has to do; he will never have peace until you let him go and learn to live again. Brian gave you many wonderful gifts. He gave you unconditional love and acceptance. Through his death, he gave you the same gift you gave him at his birth; he gave you life. He wants you to be happy. But, what you do with your life from this point on is entirely up to you; you no longer have Brian to lean on. Brian will never be more than a thought away—but he is not alive. Your older children, Ian, your grandchildren, your family and friends—they're the ones living, now's the time to enjoy them. Remember, Brian's doing fine right where he is. He doesn't need to be mothered any longer."

Dorothy's words of wisdom helped me greatly. She was right. I had needed Brian; I had built my life around him from the moment I set eyes on him. More than that, I had trained everyone I loved to make Brian the center of their lives too. If they didn't, then I simply shut them out of my life. Only those who gave of themselves to make Brian the center of my world could get close to me.

Now each day I ask God to show me the way, to lead me down the path of my own life. I also thank God each day for the gift of Brian in my life. Then I thank Brian for restoring my life to me and I ask him to help me find my way. I ask him to give me the strength and the courage to help other learning-disabled and troubled youths to find their way in the world.

I still have bad days and good days and I still do dumb things and great things. I move ahead and I go back, but the going back is less frequent now than the moving ahead. And I've learned to enjoy my life again. Most of all I've learned that I'm needed. I am needed very much by all who love me, when I take the time to include them in my world—in Brian's World.

I can now put things in perspective. I now know that every time I see an eagle overhead it isn't Brian. But the spirit of an eagle reminds me of the love and courage Brian had all his life. And as the eagle soars through the sky powering his way past foe and storm, so Brian had to find his way through many hardships during his short life.

Shortly after my talk with Dorothy, I was walking the dogs on a quiet ocean beach on Vancouver Island. I looked out at the sea and endless sky, both of which Brian loved so much. He was always so at ease with the sea. Sometimes he used to scare me for he would just go out and out, always moving further away from shore. As I stood between sea and land, I was overwhelmed by the urge to let Brian know I was there. So I set to work placing rocks and writing "HELLO BRIAN" on that lonely beach while the tide slowly crept in to the shore. I finished and looked out to where the ocean met the sky and became one. I felt so very close to my son. I felt he was there with me saying, "Hello to you too, Mom. Enjoy the rest of your life."

It was a wonderful, peaceful moment which, though over in a second, will stay with me a lifetime. Then I turned and slowly walked up the beach to my hotel to read and meditate. Knowing that I had finally said goodbye.

If I Could See You Again:
Messages From Family And Friends

In death as in life Brian was surrounded by many
friends whose lives he touched in many different ways.

If I could See You Again:
Messages from Family and Friend

Life goes on, there are lessons to be learned.

As I wrote this book, I tried to keep in mind the knowledge that God never sends us more than we can handle. I expect always to remember the pain, anguish, sadness and helplessness of being pre-deceased by my child. I will never forget my dear friend Christine speaking softly into my ear, "Brian died." But neither will I forget the words of my friend Margaret who once said, "You'll always have a teenaged son Kathy, so you're the lucky one." And I believe that out of all that grief cam great amounts of compassion, wisdom, and love for others.

Through all life's harsh lessons, these inspirational words taken from "*What a Wonderful World*" by Anne Murray bring me peace of mind:

> *Every life has a plan though sometimes the map is out of our hands.*
> *Every day is a step though we may not know the reason just yet.*

I've been told that time heals all wounds, but as each day passes the sadness of losing Brian is still with me. I often ask myself if it will ever go away. But I already know the answer to my own question. By listening to my fellow Compassionate Friends, some of whom, like Dorothy, have lost children more recently than I lost Brian and others, like Arlene, Karen, and Carol whose children died several years ago, I have learned that the answer is the same for us all. No, the pain and grief you feel over the loss of your child never goes away, but it will get easier to bear. They've told me the pain gets less with the years. There will be good days and bad days, good months and unbearable months, but through the years, we all have our precious memories to cling to.

Memories of my son, Brian, are so dear to my heart. I know I will cherish them all the days of my life. Although Brian no longer resides here on earth with all his loved ones, his love continues. All I have to do is look out at the beauty of this great big world to know that no matter what or where my child, their brother, their grandson, nephew, friend may be, he will remain forever in our hearts. And the love Brian sends down from Heaven to each and every one of us is ours to hold on to.

Many of Brian's friends and relatives had things left unsaid, feelings but vaguely felt and good-byes never expressed. The following are a few of these good-byes expressed through poems, letters, and cards for us all to read. Because of the large response, we were unable to print all the good-byes sent to us. We also had to edit some of the letters for brevity. We apologize to those whose letters we were unable to print in their entirety, but we want you all to know that the complete collection of letters and poems is tucked safely away in the toe of Brian's much-loved five-foot Christmas stocking which hangs on the back of his bedroom door, where it will remain.

Thank you to everyone who was able to contribute to this final chapter. We also want to thank those of you who phoned to say that it was still too difficult to express your feelings in writing. A special thank you to Brian's friend, who shall remain anonymous, who phoned to tell me she had written a poem for Brian which she reads often to him and was not ready to share. I'm grateful, as I'm sure Brian is, to all those friends and family members who still take the time to say hello and have a friendly conversation with him. I know he hears us all no matter how we choose to keep in touch with him.

The following letters, poems, and cards are in random order.

Dear Brian,

Even though you were given to us for such a short time, you have taught me a very valuable lesson: Life is too short and precious to waste. You need to make every minute count and live each day as best as you can. Thank you for helping me see that. I am very honored that your mom chose me to be your Godmother, I only wish I was there for you and your mom more. When things get rough and I'm not sure what to do, or my children are having a hard time, I think of you and know that any problem can be worked out, if given time, patience, and understanding. Thank you for being my nephew.

I love you and miss you very much.

Love, Your Godmother,
Aunt Pam

Hi Brian,

This isn't an easy letter to write. (What would I like to say to you if I have just five minutes of your time?)

See, the problem is since your untimely death I have spent much time talking with you. When you were here on earth with us we really never saw much of you after you moved from Hemmingford to Prince Albert at about five years old. Before that you were just a little boy in his white suit.

We have videotapes of your modeling—I like the car commercial best—and now of your mom's TV interviews to help keep your memory alive. We always followed your life's ups and downs through your mom's joys and concerns. That is not the same as actually living the experience with you. You can never fully appreciate what someone is experiencing without being there.

We are very proud of your mother for the strength she has shown to keep going through all of the tragedy and still be able to help others the way she has. God willing, and with your help, she will continue.

Please keep those "miracles" happening and I will always continue talking to you.

Love, till we meet again,
Gram K.

Brian,

If I could see you one more time, I guess I wouldn't have too much to say. I mean, you know I love you and miss you terribly, and you also know we'll see each other again. I would imagine time goes by pretty quickly in Heaven, so you're the one with less time to wait. I guess I'd just want to give you a hug and say, "Be patient, Snuggles, we'll all see you soon!"

And Brian, practice your b-ball; you're gonna need it if you EVER want to beat me!

Love,
Jessica Bard

If I had five minutes to talk to Brian before he died, knowing that he would be gone in five minutes, there is no doubt as to what I would say to him. I would ask him if he knew, I mean really knew beyond a shadow of a doubt that he would be in Heaven with Jesus when he died. If he said yes, I would ask him how he knows.

We could discuss all the wonders of Heaven. No more disabilities or unkind people, only happiness and joy. Of a light that didn't come from one source, like the sun, but it came from the glory of God, from every direction. We would rejoice in the journey that Brian was about to undertake.

I love you Brian,
Aunt Linda

Poem given to me by the staff at Kamloops Safe House; author unknown:

My dearest family some things I'd like to say but first of all to let you know that I arrived okay I'm writing this from Heaven where I dwell with God above where there's no more tears or sadness there is just eternal love Please do not be unhappy just because I'm out of sight remember that I'm with you every morning, noon and night. That day I had to leave you, when my life on Earth was through, God picked me up and hugged me and said I welcome you. It's good to have you back again; you were missed while you were gone, as for your dearest family they'll be here later on.

I need you here so badly as part of my big plan, there's so much that we have to do to help our mortal man. Then God gave me a list of things He wished for me to do, and foremost on that list of mine is to watch and take care of you. And I will be beside you every day and week and year, and when you're sad, I'm standing there to wipe away the tear. And when you lie in bed at night, the day's chores put to flight, God and I are closest to you in the middle of the night. So when you think of my life on Earth and all those loving years, because you're only human they are bound to bring you tears. But do not be afraid to cry, it does relieve the pain, remember there would be no flowers, unless there was some rain.

I wish that I could tell you of all that God has planned, but if I were to tell you, you wouldn't understand. But one thing is for certain, though my life on Earth is over, I am closer to you now than I ever was before. And to my very many friends, trust God knows what is best. I'm still not far away from you; I'm just beyond the crest. There are rocky roads ahead of you, and many hills to climb, but together we can do it taking one day at a time. It was always my philosophy and I'd like it for you too, that as you give unto the World so will the World give back to you. If you can help somebody who is in sorrow or in pain, then you can say to God at night my day was not in vain. And now I am contented that my life is worthwhile, knowing as I passed along the way I made somebody smile. So if you meet somebody who is down and feeling low, just lend a hand to pick him up as on your way you go. When you are walking down the street and you've got me on your mind, I'm walking in your footsteps only half a step behind. And when you feel the gentle breeze or the wind upon your face, its me giving you a great big hug or just a soft embrace. And when it's time for you to go from that body to be free, remember you're not going you are coming here to me. And I will always love you from that land way up above. We'll be in touch again soon.

PS God sends His Love.

Card given by Brian's friend Jess "Protal Card" (La Dolce Vita 225 f4031 God's Porch)
The card reads as follows:

God's Porch

If I could sit across the porch from God,
I'd thank Him for the glory of morning,
and for starry skies. I'd thank him for
the magic of a child's soft smile, for memories,
and for this wonderful feeling we call love.
I'd thank him for the hopes
and dreams of this sweet life. And most
of all, I'd thank him for lending me you.
I miss you Brian, and I love you as much as ever.
Jess

(The envelope read: To Brian c/o Heaven. Love Jess)

Dear Brian,

Your mom asked us to think about what we would say to you if we were given five minutes. I've given it a lot of thought. Being that I talk fast, I could say lots, but would it have any lasting meaning?

I didn't know you very well. By the time you were born, you lived away and I figured you already knew what a great disciplinarian I was. That explains the past.

Now for the present. If there is one thing I've learned in this life, it is not to judge others unless you are perfect (I'm not even close)

I won't pretend to be familiar with the details of your life, but I understand you caused your mom more than the average number of stressful moments. I do know that in your death you gave your mother two of the greatest gifts of all, pride in her son and peace in her heart.

Your mom knows that you made it through the tough times to reach a place in your life where you were ready and able to help others. God must have needed you very badly to put you through so many tests, getting you ready to be with him so soon.

I hope one day to see you again and say, "Hey Brian, I'm your Aunt Connie and I love you." Now, as I said, I talk pretty fast so this should take about two minutes, with your other three go talk and laugh with your friends. I know you have many of them and know we are proud of you.

Love, Aunt Connie

Hey, what's up? Thought you were dead. Anyway, thank you for the little trick you and Darren played on me, it was fun. We had a lot of fun while we knew each other. Oh, thanks for offering me a place to stay when I was on the streets.

From
Aaron

If I Only Knew

I would have told you all the things I never found the time to. The things I thought I'd have a lifetime to say. Like I loved the time we spent together when you were little, building many fond memories: dressing you up, playing peek-a-boo, holidays, birthdays and many many more.

As I got older I spent less and less time with you because I was too involved in my own life: school, work, friends and then my family. (Not knowing I wasn't going to have forever to make up for lost time.)

Then it was your turn to be wrapped up in friends, school and work. (But who would have known we were losing precious time?)

Taylor was the most fortunate of my children because he got to spend a lot of time with you building wonderful memories to share with his brothers.

Joshua and Zachary had the misfortune of not getting to know you. But Taylor, Alain and I have many memories to share with them so they too can get to know who you were.

Rebecca.

A light went out
The other night
And all the while I cried.
It just flickered out of sight
And to help it no one tried

But just for a second's pause
The galaxies stopped singing.
It screamed one scream
In evils claws,
Heaven echoed with its ringing

Then quickly angels flew about
And birthed a brand new star.
It's not the same, I tried to shout,
But the heavens were too far.

It will never be the same
Without you Brian. We love
You and we'll always hold
Our memories of you close to
Our heart. You're with God now.

Jessica Bard.

One sad day you went away
As tears fill my eyes
I regret the event of your demise
Loved by so many missed so much.

Pain and tears touch you no more
As I sit here I remember
Your laugh, smile and touch
And our ongoing fight of Nike and Fabu

You were young much too young to go
Your road too long and time too short
God knew your pain
So he took you away from us all

Brian, I know one day
When I see you again you'll open your arms
And show me the way
Until this day I'll wait as I pray

Our ages identical
And friends the same
I'm sorry I never told you how awesome you are
So until you wake again I love you and goodbye.

Love, Brenda

Dear Brian,

I wish I could have known you, the person inside, that is my biggest regret. I remember when you were about two or three years old, your mom used to dress you in the most adorable outfits. What a handsome little boy! I remember that best because we usually saw you on special occasions, like Easter and Christmas.

I'm sure I don't have to tell you that your mom adored you. She would have done anything in the Universe for you. She could not have loved you more than she did.

Your older brother, Mike, and I are about the same age and your sister, Becky, is eleven months younger than I am. Mike and I were in the same kindergarten class; that was the year he and I had the chicken pox at the same time. We were plastered with them. Becky and I played together a lot. I remember how she liked beautiful dolls and things that were frilly and lacy. I liked matchbox cars and getting dirty. What a combination, huh!

I wish I had been a bigger part of your life even if it had only been over the phone. You were dealt a very complicated hand of cards at a very early age. I'm not going to say that I understand anything that you endured, because I couldn't possibly imagine what life was like in your shoes. You made some unwise decisions that lead you down a path of wrong turns. Some choices caused your loved ones many sleepless nights, I'm sure, but I won't judge you by your actions nor should anyone else. You were only a child and children make mistakes, some bigger than others, but they all make mistakes.

You never met my son. His name is Josh; he was born in 1990 so he is ten years old now. He likes to ride on anything with a motor. His favorite is his snowmobile; he'll stay on that till he runs out of gas. I also have a fiancé, his name is Stacey and he is a tree surgeon. We've been engaged for quite a while.

I will leave you with this short message: Brian, you are in a better place now with God, He created Brian's World and will understand it better than this society that we live in. You will live on in the hearts of all who love and care about you.

Goodbye Brian
Love,
Aunt Josette

Brian,

You left way too soon, and I miss you. Since you left I took a long, hard look at my life and realized I needed to make some changes. Thank you for giving me the strength I needed to go on, and make my life better.

I wish you could be here to see but I know you're looking down and with a smile on your face, you see me doing good. I dedicate this to you. I love ya Brian.

Amber-dawn Bard
2000

Brian, (if I had five minutes to speak with you)

I am so happy for you. It's a wonderful thing to love your job and British Columbia is Beautiful. It is very sad, your leaving us, I will try to fit as much in as possible as I say goodbye.

First remember that you will always shine in your mother's eyes. Moms are like that, she will never be able to let you go whether you're physically here or not. Take with you also that families always have a special bond even if you don't see them every week, or every month or even every year, that bond always remains. I know you haven't seen us in years so I will fill you in—my son Jordan is now nearly sixteen years old. You can definitely tell that the two of you are related, you have similar looks. We just bought a house that is one hundred and thirty years old—it has a lot of history to it (and a lot of work).

I wish you could be with us at the upcoming family reunion, but I know you will be there in spirit.

Aunt Judy

Dear Brian,

I am so happy to have one last chance to talk with you. You left us so suddenly I never had a chance to tell you how proud I am that you straightened out your life and got back on the right track. I never had much chance to do things with you as you lived so far away. I would have liked to have taken you to a ball game or hockey game as I have my grandsons that live close by, or maybe we could have gone fishing or hunting together as you got older. Most of all I would have loved the opportunity to see you up in the logging camp and had you show me the helicopter operation. I have always wanted to ride in a helicopter; maybe you could have arranged it. I know we can never do any of these things, but you will always be in my heart. Now we have to say good-bye and will you always keep me in your prayers until we meet again.

Love, Gramp

Hey, you little shit, how's it goin'? Tell me, why'd you have to go and do a thing like that, leave us all here while you take off to have fun in Heaven. I was just wondering, are there car races and Harleys up there? How are the girls? Cute, I bet! Anyway, just wanted you to know I miss ya lots and wish we had had more time together. Hey, try and stay out of trouble for a while will ya, and stay put so we can find ya when we get there.
   Catch ya later

Love, Mike

PS Fatboy (Cody) and Dude (Nikki) send their love too! They say, "Tell Uncle Brian we love him lots!"

To my friend in Heaven
Brian,

I'm sitting here on this lonely earth wondering why it's always the good people that have to go. I remember the first time I met you at "The Slate" with Amber. Right away I could tell that you were a good guy. We started hanging out and became really good friends, inseparable, cruising around, having fun. Brian, I wish I could change that first day that we decided to do drugs, I think about it every single day and wonder that maybe if I hadn't convinced you that maybe things would be different now. I was caught up in the wrong life-style and I dragged you down with me. For that I can never forgive myself, ever! But regardless you stuck by me through thick and thin like a true friend. People like you are hard to come by Brian, you were one of a kind! There are so many things I wish I could change about the way we were, I regret that whole year, but I guess all I can do is change my present and look into the future. I know you are watching down on us all, I can feel it like a presence up above guiding us all. I owe you the biggest apology Brian, I'm so sorry that I ever brought you down. Words can't describe my remorse. What I can do though Brian, is let your memory bring me up and guide me. I never saw you near the end, but I was told you turned your life around. Now it's my turn to do that, and I'll do it for you. I owe you at least that much and I'm sure it's what you would want. So, keep watching over us all Brian, your memory will always live on. Don't forget to save a space up there for me, because one day we'll see each other again, this time in a place of happiness and freedom. Goodbye my friend, I miss you!

Love,
Darren Burry

To an Angel

My heavenly friend
Sitting so high up there,
Finally at peace,
No more pain or despair.

My heavenly friend
Whom I knew for not too long,
Forgive me Brian Roberts,
Forever leading you wrong.

My heavenly friend
My heart aches in pain,
If I had just one wish,
It would be to see you once again.

I would tell you what's been killing me
The thoughts that are in my head,
The things that I convinced you to do,
It should be me that is dead.

My heavenly friend,
As I kneel here on my knees,
I pray and pray that one great day,
Brian, forgive me please?

My heavenly friend,
Sometimes I dream that you're still here,
As I'm walking down the street,
You will suddenly appear.

You tell me to look at myself
And what I have become,
Tell me that I need some help,
And that's why you have come.

You tell me that I can change,
Learn to look beyond the past.
"Live for the future," you said,
"quit living life so fast."

And in that dream you walked away,
With a final goodbye, you turned around.
"Follow God," you said, "He won't lead you astray,
Seek not, my friend, for He is finally found."

I sat there dazed when I woke up
Making sense of what I'd heard.
When I heard the sound of wings
Fluttering like a bird.

You were the Angel, Brian,
Come to tell me what to do,
I'll pay heed to what you said,
Because nothing could be more true.

To me that dream was more than real
I sat in my bed and cried,
It gave me the only chance
I'd have to say goodbye.

My friend who art in Heaven,
You are my soul, my guiding light,
Your memory will always live on,
Like a star shining bright up in the sky.

Someday we will meet again,
When I too will die.
But until that fateful day does come,
My heavenly friend, goodbye.

Forgive me Brian, I miss you
Love your friend,
Darren

Brian,

If I could see you again I would tell you how much I miss you and how my plans for the future with you were destroyed. I always looked forward to the time when you outgrew your rebellious stage and settled down. I looked forward to doing many things with you. Some as simple as just sitting around talking, to going on trips, and even working on projects. I always believed that you could do anything you wanted to and looked forward to being part of your ultimate success. I will always miss you as I wonder what would you have become, and I miss being part of it.

Love,
Dad

Why?
When I wake up each morning and look out at the bright blue sky
To anyone who's listening, I always ask why
Why my son, why my child?
Why anyone's child, why do they have to die?

Who makes the rules?
Who chooses who's to live and who's to die?
What lessons are we to learn?
By the loss of our precious little one

Why do birds go on singing?
Why does the sun shine its bright sunny rays?
Why does the moon smile down each lonely night?
Why does everyone's life go on while mine stands so still?

I've often wondered why a sweet young child should die
Why not take burglars, thieves and chimpanzees
Why take our children so dear to our heart
Then I realize we're all somebody's children right from the start

So each night as I go to bed I say a prayer
I thank God for the gift of you in my life
You'll be with me always, my guiding light
You're still my child, my angel, my life

I will close Brian's story with words of wisdom from a very special child in my life, my Grandson, Taylor. During Christmas 1999 while watching his favorite television program, he summed up the meaning of loss. Despite the happy scene taking place on the television, one of the characters on the screen was crying. Little Taylor asked his mom, "Why are they crying when there is nothing wrong and they should be happy?"

"Well, Taylor, sometimes people are so happy they cry."

Taylor sat and thought about that for a moment, then he said, "Do you know what would make me so happy I would cry, Mom?"

"No, Taylor," replied Becky. "What would make you so happy you would cry?"

"If I saw my Uncle Brian on this earth again it would make me so happy I would cry."

Taylor was seven years old at the time, but what a powerful statement he made. For isn't it true for all of us that to see a lost child again on this earth, even for only a moment, would make us so happy we would cry?

I understand the long hard road I have traveled. I know where I am today in my life, in my faith and in my world but I do not know where tomorrow will lead me. So, I live my life the best way I know, with unconditional love and acceptance for all I meet as I continue my journey, one day at a time.

To all of you with troubled hearts, may you find the courage and strength to go on living. May you then find the added strength to help someone else in their struggle to overcome the darkness.

This book is dedicated to all of our children—loved, lost, remembered.

0-595-30434-6